Citizen, Citizenship and Awareness of Citizenship

I0121144

Fikret Çelik

Citizen, Citizenship and Awareness of Citizenship

**Intellectual, Political, and Social Debates
in the Historical and Theoretical Framework
for the Western Citizenship Case**

PETER LANG

**Bibliographic Information published by the
Deutsche Nationalbibliothek**
The Deutsche Nationalbibliothek lists this publication in the Deutsche
Nationalbibliografie; detailed bibliographic data is available online at
http://dnb.d-nb.de.

Library of Congress Cataloging-in-Publication Data
A CIP catalog record for this book has been applied for at the
Library of Congress.

ISBN 978-3-631-84001-6 (Print)
E-ISBN 978-3-631-84212-6 (E-PDF)
E-ISBN 978-3-631-84213-3 (EPUB)
E-ISBN 978-3-631-84214-0 (MOBI)
DOI 10.3726/b17851

© Peter Lang GmbH
Internationaler Verlag der Wissenschaften
Berlin 2020
All rights reserved.

Peter Lang – Berlin · Bern · Bruxelles · New York · Oxford · Warszawa · Wien

This publication has been peer reviewed.

www.peterlang.com

Contents

Preamble

The foundations of all the scientific and social phenomena discussed in the Western world today can be reduced to the Ancient Greek civilization. For this reason, it is seen that a lot of the current political phenomena and even the discussions that address the classification and conceptualization stand in front of us, not only today, but also in a way that the history can be taken back two thousand five centuries. It is an undeniable fact that human beings, as a political and social entity, are considered as "individuals" with their rights and responsibilities in the modern period, depending on the understanding of the Ancient Greek, in the context of "citizen" and "citizenship".

The change and transformation that the Western people had undergone throughout the Middle Ages, Renaissance, and Enlightenment periods, naturally also had an impact on the understanding of citizen and citizenship. But especially in the XIX and XX centuries, with the influence of modernism and developing ideologies, the citizen came to the fore as a legal, economic, and technological entity as well as a political and social individual. With the effect of the general acceptance of the Representative democracy in the Western world in the modern period, the citizen became the most important subject in politics and therefore in the states. This process has now become a key factor in determining the future of countries, along with their obligations and rights. The period when the citizen became the most important subject of the political system also expressed in a process that includes many paradoxes in the world, such as capitalism and socialism, in the ideologies that try to shape and determine the individual and society from their own perspective.

Citizenship has been an important subject of politics and social sciences in the ancient, modern, and post-modern eras that I have tried to emphasize above, and it is still in this position. It is certain that there will be more discussion on citizenship.

The situation that prompted me to work on such a subject is a study with a theoretical and practical dimension called "*A Research on Researching the Awareness of Citizenship: A Case of Kırıkkale Province*" that I conducted as a scientific research project at Kırıkkale University as a project manager. It is the case that this study, which comes to the forefront as a research of field, has the technical dimension with a sample area, shows me that the civic debates and literature are at least theoretically insufficient at the point of "awareness of citizenship". For this reason, I have wanted to make a study including the developments in the historical process and theoretical discussions in order to understand the current situation on citizenship and citizenship consciousness by making use of the theoretical part of this study and the extensive readings I have made on the subject. In my study, I thought that it should be seen the places of the important writers and thinkers of the ancient, modern and post-modern eras in the discussions on behalf of citizenship from their point of view (especially over the important personalities of the modern and post-modern era). While trying to remind the ideas put forward by the classical political thinkers (Aristotle, Cicero, Machiavelli, Hobbes, etc.) here, I have found it appropriate to make a study based on the discussions of modern and post-modern period writers and thinkers, who are considered important on citizenship, within the framework of the ideas of classical thinkers. Thus, I have opened up to discussion the views of contemporary writers and thinkers who deal with the views of classical thinkers who treat the issue of citizens and citizenship at certain points. While looking at the discussions on this issue, I tried to broaden the context within the framework of the concept of "awareness of citizenship" in the hope of a better understanding of citizen and citizenship that modern period changes and transforms. Having limited to the Western world for the theoretical and historical debates that I dealt with the dimension of awareness of citizenship and without entering into citizenship discussions in Turkey, I just wanted to contribute to the literature for citizenship debates to be based on a theoretical and historical context only in Turkey.

Additionally, I followed a literature review within the study that includes the general academic assumptions about the subject and different interpretations/definitions of citizenship and that contains the comparison of the different perspectives on the subject of the opinions of the important individuals whose views are dominant on this subject. Besides, I was involved in the discussions with my own views many times in the text, and at some points, I tried to expand the discussion points on the subject of "awareness of citizenship" by adding my own views on the theoretical and practical dimension of the subject.

I would like to thank my dear wife Dr. Vasfiye ÇELIK, who does not withhold support from me despite her intense academic studies, and my daughter Fatma Zeynep ÇELIK, who does not miss her smile even though I neglect her from time to time. Also thanks my dear brother and colleague Assoc. Dr. Yusuf SAYIN, who are a faculty member of the Department of Political Science and International Relations of Necmettin Erbakan University and who has very important contributions in the English writing of this book.

Eskisehir, September/2020

Abstract It is observed that human beings are evaluated in terms of citizens and citizenship together with their "rights" and "responsibilities" during the process from the formation inherited from the Ancient Greek to its modern version. In this sense, by the 17th century and the Age of Enlightenment, the new meanings that citizenship gained within the framework of modern principles and values are important in affecting the present day. With this process, it is certain that the most important contribution of the modern era to citizenship is its evaluation as a "conscious being". Citizenship has thus become an important area of discussion in political theory through the phenomena of "equality", "freedom", "sovereignty", "solidarity", "participation", and "welfare". These debates have not lost anything of their academic and intellectual appeal in the post-modern era in which we are. However, it is a fact that the effects of the adventure of the individual to be a citizen as a conscious being firstly on the Western civilization and then on the world people have gained a different dimension with today's unpredictable developments. At this point, the views of the important writers and intellectuals of the modern and post-modern period, and the new and at the same time, "hybrid" political and social theories are discussed in different dimensions of citizenship thought. This book can be regarded as an important attempt to clearly determine the place of all problem areas related to citizenship in current political and social theories through these discussions.

Keywords: Civic, citizenship, awareness of citizenship, political and social rights, modern period, post-modern period, welfare state

Introduction

*"Throughout much of the recorded history, the
claim that adults have the right to be treated
as political equals was clearly absurd, and the
rulers regarded it as a dangerous and destructive
demand.*

*The spread of democratic thoughts and beliefs
since the 18th century turned this devastating
demand into ordinary demand; so much so that,
in practice, authoritarian rulers who completely
rejected this claim embraced the claim in their
public statements.*

*Nevertheless, even in democratic countries, every
citizen who carefully observes political realities
can conclude that there is a big gap between the
target of political equality and its practice. In some
democratic countries, including the United States,
this gap is growing steadily and seems to be at risk
of losing the ideal of equality altogether". (Dahl,
2018: 13).*

While this danger really constitutes an important problem for democracy
and the acceptance of its legitimacy in today's world, many recent political developments have paved the way for the increasing the necessary
interest towards the fact of citizenship and the norms addressed within
this context. At this point, some developments have been observed. Such
reasons as the lack of political electoral indifference (depoliticization)
experienced in some countries, the rise of nationalism in various parts of
Europe and the failures of citizens' activities in the context of movements
such as environmentalism have brought up the re-evaluation of citizenship today in a way that covers many problem areas (Daunhauer, 2001).

While reconsidering citizenship, it is necessary to review the evolution
that it has undergone in the modern period, in a different dimension from
the ancient period. Because today an understanding such as citizen and
human be separately handled has been encountered. This situation is due

to an important transformation in the modern era. This development can also be characterized as a result of a transformation of political and social phenomena. According to some recent thinkers, this transformation is a result of being evaluated as "the necessity of collective or general interest to override private interest". In this way the citizen in the modern period has become both an entity reinforced by a common force and an assured person of social rights (Jaume, 2003: 992). This understanding has led to a situation of redefinition of the citizen with certain characteristics "as an anthropological concept that defines it as a political entity in active participation in public life", which can be taken back to the Renaissance in a general framework, when the ancient period is based on. In this way when the citizen is considered as a phenomenon, citizenship is revealed as a position that becomes possible "when it is underlined that it can only be possible in a collective life and by forming a space of freedom owned by the fates and passions of people" (Spitz, 2003: 997–998). At this point, in order to determine the position of citizenship, the evolution between the state and the citizen has been seen to be important. In this sense, Gianfranco Poggi made the following determination:

> "The state is no longer identical to society, as in ancient Greek *politea*. Citizens' commitment to the welfare and security of the state is no longer ensured by their personal commitment to a leader. Duties with certain political responsibilities and powers are not distributed according to wealth, social position or religious beliefs. The growing scope, costs, and increasing efficiency of the state are now covered by a state budget enriched by taxes collected from citizens' income and expenditure, not by donating money from people, selling some authorities, selling shares gained from wars and colonialism or spending personal assets... the state constitutes a framework for the citizens of the state to protect their private interests that are completely different from each other. Its demands from individuals can be heavy (such as participating in wars); however, its approach to the individual is different and it is within the framework of an abstract citizen concept (1991: 99)".

The citizenship, which emerges as a concept that determines the place of human beings as a political and social entity in various ways as an individual within the framework of certain definitions and relations from the ancient times until today as a part of the historical adventure of the West in this way, is also the name of the individual becoming a strong figure as a legal, political, and economic entity against the state today. In this context, it is important to determine the position of the citizen as a political phenomenon or to determine the position of the human being in the society with the political systems as an entity becoming aware of its rights and responsibilities as a strong individual. In this context, it is essential to discuss the debates about citizenship in theory and practice together. Because today, all the discussions on a political and social basis constitute the most important areas of discussion about how far the practice and theory can compromise each other, how much they can meet each other, and how parallel they are with each other.

While it is possible to deal with citizenship discussions within the framework of this perspective, it is attempted to understand what the link between nation-states and citizenship that left their mark on the 21st century has become by the increasing globalization in the discussions taking place from a different or newer perspective. In this point of view, it is thought that the link between the state and the citizen began to break in the global age. Additionally, with the increasing importance of globalization on social and political phenomena, the nation-state system has begun to be seen as an obstacle to political participation and started to be criticized. With such discussions, the concepts within the framework of *"denationalization of citizenship"* have been brought to the fore, and new discussion areas have been formed on how to open the way of *"political participation"* for the citizen as a conscious entity at this point (Kadıoğlu, 2008a). In this context, starting from the words of Dahrendorf, Colin Crouch, which emphasizes the new situation waiting for the citizen in the globalized world today saying *"we have stepped into a new area that we can define as post-democracy"*; it seems to have brought an important issue to the agenda *"...by traditional methods invented for the aims to be achieved – through parliamentary elections–, obviously these goals will no longer be achieved. The problem regarding the future of democracy... the problem of how we will meet the (new) requirements is present: The issue of public speaking..."* (2015: 73).

In order to be able to identify the areas of discussion about citizenship, which we briefly mentioned above, there are a lot of ambiguous political and social contexts that we can evaluate over what can be done and not done in order to raise awareness of citizens in this new world as well as in many respects, including a paradoxical situation. In this context, it is clear that the national one has some political and ideological impacts on the global and the national on the global, even when it is considered superficially. Therefore, there is sufficient evidence to show that the historical process that citizenship has undergone theoretically and practically should be subject to many discussions on behalf of the political and social sciences.

This study aims to reveal the intellectual, political, social, and economic dimensions of the citizenship phenomenon and the debates within the framework of a process as above, together with the developments in the ancient, modern, and post-modern period, with its present unclear problem areas. The study also deals the discussions experienced in many aspects on this phenomenon in Turkey with the development of the phenomenon of citizenship in political, social, and legal; the text has been presented to the reader in three main sections, considering a historical and related intellectual development sequence. In the study, using the detailed explanation footnotes of important facts, events, and people related to the subject, efforts have been made to prevent the fluency of the main text to be interrupted at minimum.

The first part of the study, which is based on the structure explained above, focuses on the historical and theoretical explanation of the phenomenon of citizenship, and it is primarily aimed to evaluate the cases of citizens and citizenship in a detailed way in the conceptual framework in this context. Here, the subject is dealt with in terms of clarifying or determining the conceptual framework through the phenomena that form definitions and discussions about citizens and citizenship in today's context. Later, this chapter includes the dimensions of political thoughts, political history, and historical sociology. From the Ancient Greek until the 20th century and along with the political, economic, and social dimensions, it is tried to present the adventure in the West regarding citizens and citizenship with the historical range and theoretical discussions. In this regard, the historical process of citizenship is evaluated primarily from the discussions on equality, freedom, and the being political and non-political views of the Ancient Greek civilization under the framework of the views of various classical schools of thought and their thinkers. In accordance with the purpose of the study; the views of classical thinkers are tried to be handled within the discussions of contemporary writers on the subject of citizenship discussions. For this reason; the opinions, which are put forward by the classical writers on behalf of citizenship, (as an option), are examined through the studies of contemporary writers, thinkers, and academicians who addressed them in their evaluations on this subject. The discussions in the historical dimension within the framework of the phenomenon of citizenship are handled at the point of development from the Ancient Greek to Rome and tried to be evaluated from the point of view of new perspectives emerging from the predominantly Christian thought. At the end of the first chapter; with the dimensions that reached the modern era from the Middle Ages, the cases coming to the fore through citizenship are analyzed in detail at the point of the opinions of thinkers shaping the history of political thought and in determining political and social developments on behalf of the Western world.

The second chapter of the book discusses how to form citizenship in a meaningful way through the "awareness of citizenship", including the modern period, and in the guidance of determination of political and social rights. In this context, the formation and development of citizens in the context of modern nation-state and modern values are tried to be evaluated from many dimensions. This chapter evaluates, basically, the effects of the developments in the pre-modern, modern and occasional times on the understanding of the dimensions of various paradoxical, ambiguous, and eclectic debates on the phenomenon of citizenship in detail. Within this framework, this political and social based theoretical discussion takes the important thinkers and philosophers' views on the formation/constitution of "awareness of citizenship" through primary and secondary sources. The process taking place until the post-modern era is not ignored in historical developments, and the subject is tried to examine such subjects as nation, nation-state, sovereignty, patriotism, social welfare state, and social and political rights for the modern period. In this context, theoretical debates are sometimes considered as the historical backward and forward evaluation of the leading events on some cases.

The third part of the study mentions about the evaluating of the redefinition of today's citizenship through interests and understanding of equality, it makes detailed discussions over "awareness of citizenship", which develops under the influence of these facts, through the meanings of the era of globalization. At this point, in addition to such concepts as nation-state, patriotism, social and political rights, which are also discussed in the some places of second chapter, many areas or facts of problem like identity, social corporatism, multiculturalism, community, social justice, migration/immigration, liberal-individualist understanding, republicanism and neo-liberalism/neo-conservatism, which are complementary to the modern era and definitive of the post-modern era, are opened for discussion, taking into account some practices experienced in the Western predecessor countries through citizenship and awareness of citizenship. In these discussions, the views of important writers, thinkers, and academics, whose determinative effect is known in the formation of the Western literature especially from the last quarter of the 20th century to the present, are discussed in detail from primary and secondary sources. The study results in an evaluation trying to analyze the entire text and specifically developed based on "awareness of citizenship".

I Citizen and Citizenship as a Theoretical and Historical Case

Citizenship, which is considered as one of the specific premise cases for political theory and sociology, also has a vital importance for the whole of the literature of social sciences as a concept. Because, "citizenship", at the point of evaluating issues such as "nature of democratic participation", "analyzing social rights", "legitimacy of the people", and "understanding the nature of the state for human societies", which are important political and social debate areas for modern societies today, is considered as a key concept (Turner & Hamilton, 1994: I).

Considering these dimensions today; according to Dauenhauer, the phenomenon of citizenship, which seems to be able to be carried out on the discussions that enable it to be understood more clearly, is one of the important debate areas in the history of the Western political thought from past to present. Although it has naturally undergone some changes in the historical process, it has always been tried to define citizenship, "which always includes the purpose of adding the requirements of justice to the needs of a community or community membership", as "closely related to the ideas of both individual rights and commitment to a particular community" (2001). Citizenship, which is handled over the rights and obligations of Dauenhauer, complementing this understanding by Skeat, is considered as a city-related entity, and also defined as a "living in a city" in accordance with its Latin and Greek origins (1985: 111). When considered in terms of political origin, with this urban emphasis, the way in which citizenship debates are handled in conjunction with the Ancient Greek has been a turning point in the emergence of the Western political thoughts. Here, the citizen became an important phenomenon in the Greek city-state tradition on issues such as "democracy" and "criticism of democracy" discussed with "talent". These democracy debates have later important functions to reveal the "elite" debates and the position of those having the power in the city, with the exception of those holding power, together with the question of whom would have the power to rule; that is, it has occupied an important place in the understanding of the position of "a large non-wealthy social group" in urban life in the political sense. It is thought to be an important tension in the Ancient Greek, especially in the implementation/practicing of politics, research, and understanding of various models of democracy. It is one of the general admissions today that issues such as the handling of democracy models that are suitable for society/societies in a "critical" framework always constitute a problem area for the continuation of the political order in the Ancient Greek (Canfora, 2003: 38–39). According to Alain Touraine, who approached the issue within the framework of this understanding, citizenship, "even though they do not have thoughts such thoughts as common belief, general willingness, that is, the understanding of liberal democracy that respects basic human rights from Hobbes to Rousseau, is the phenomenon including thoughts that constitute the freedom of the ancients and republican understanding" (2002: 267).

When we look at the literature of sociology; citizenship, in Gordon Marshall's "Dictionary of Sociology", is defined as "a phenomenon used in political theory and law theory to understand the rights and duties of members of a nation state or city". Gordon Marshall, in the same place, historically described citizenship as "covering all the members of a city, that is, to express an urban community relatively exempt from the man-datory demands of a monarch or state". The citizen in the Classical Greek thought, according to Gordon Marshall again, is also defined as a con-cept used to express individuals in a "limited to free people who have the right to participate in political debates because they contribute directly to the city state (usually through military service)" (1999: 833). Zygmunt Bauman, on the other hand, tries to explain the citizen over "being a cit-izen" and the rights and responsibilities of the citizen, as a citizen of the state, in a way that is closer to this understanding, but from a broader perspective; "Being a citizen means having a say in determining the state policy (that is, the definition of these rights and duties) in addition to being national (a carrier of the rights and duties assigned by the state). In other words, being a citizen means having the capacity to influence the activity of the state and thus to participate in the definition and management of the "law and order" in which the state strives for protection (1999: 180)".

In "The Oxford Companion to Philosophy", edited by Ted Honderich, the citizen is portrayed as "not only a legal status, but also a normative ideal within the political philosophy". In this context, citizenship is also considered as an individual event, a "phenomenon" whose entity is accepted in "administrative activities where equal and complete participation is achieved in political processes". In this context, the citizen seen as a determinant element of democracy is also considered as a phenomenon in this work that cannot be existed in monarchy or military dictatorships together and described as an important feature of modern democracies "... as a general result of the right to participate in public life" with the effect of liberalism thought in the modern period..." (1995: 135–136). According to Richard Bellamy, citizenship, when considered as a historical entity, is defined as "having the official status of a political and legal membership – at least in the Western political tradition – and having certain rights and obligations that are separated from being subjects". At this point, according to Bellamy, who emphasizes that being a member of a society or country in the historical sense can be evaluated according to different criteria, citizenship can also be defined based on "the character of the norms and attitudes that must fulfill the rights and obligations" within the framework of the above perspective (2015: 2).

At this point, it is seen that the problem area that should be solved basically in the definition of citizenship is discussed, starting from the political origins of citizenship whether sociologically, philosophical or historical, as the issue was first addressed. It is a frequently emphasized situation in the literature that we are faced with a concept of citizenship dealt within the framework of "political equality", especially as it is intensely discussed in its modern sense today. Political equality is the most controversial issue with its positive and negative aspects of continual social stability since the Ancient Greek, and it is still not agreed upon whether it has been fully resolved or not. Robert A. Dahl's findings on what political equality in this dimension implies in the social dimension present remarkable arguments in terms of understanding the essence of citizenship debates and perceiving his claims that citizenship is a result of "human nature":

> "What is it that actually drives some people in the downstairs with the privileged layer to insist on a greater political equality? Why do the subalterns in the downstairs demand for being treated as political equal to the privileged in the upstairs who rule them? Are there aspects of 'human nature' or human abilities that can be warned and sometimes stimulated to mobilize people to make

such demands? If we assume that political equality is a justifiable goal or target for a number of reasons, but it is never a description of the actual conditions that are necessarily mandatory among people, would we have to assume that movements towards political equality are driven only by ethical concerns?... Can the quest for political equality be triggered by 'more fundamental' motives? ...At this point, it can be objected that the question of why we should pursue political equality as an aim (epistemologically and ontologically) is different from the question why some people actually pursue this goal. I think this is a just objection. We owe the clear distinction to David Hume and Immanuel Kant, aside from other thinkers, that the moral propositions how people should behave and the empirical propositions how people actually behave or tend to behave. Blurring or overlooking this distinction results in the error, which is called 'the mistake of confusing what is or should be' (2018: 37–38)".

Considering the political and legal meaning over the human nature mentioned above, political equality, which can be perceived as a reflection of an ideal of equality, becomes a more meaningful concept, when taken together with citizenship in the historical and theoretical sense. Political equality in the Ancient Greek city-state and by the Western classical political theorists for their time was considered as an important part of politics throughout the ages as a "current practical problem". From this point of view, the wars between the neighboring states that were endlessly continuing in the Greek city states and the constant conflicts between the rich and the poor revealed that the issue of citizenship as a recipe for "social peace" in the Ancient Greek thought came to the agenda. In this sense, citizenship was discussed at the point *"Was it safer to gather power in a few hands, or to dissolve it more broadly? Was it safer to make it easier for foreigners to become citizens or not?"*. Plato (427–347 BC) was found to be at an important point in discussing this question. Plato saw the tyranny of Thirty Tyrants in the city-state of Athens and personally witnessed the administration, which was called 'naive democracy' of the day, sentenced Socrates to death (469–399 BC) because he did not give up his thoughts. Therefore, Plato was involved in the citizenship debates by preaching a political system as follows and proposing a solution; "implementation of a social peace recipe based on the absolute authority of 'protectors' or 'philosopher-king'" (Miller et al., 1995: 456–457). A while after Plato put forward this view, Aristotle (384–322 BC), who is his student and one of the most important representatives of the Classical Greek thought placed the question of citizenship at the center of "social reconciliation" and "peace". According to him;

> "Political authority was in a unique position; because what is meant by political authority was the authority of civil servants over citizens according to the constitutional rules. Thus, political authority was traditional and limited; it was a form of authority that was far from the natural power of husbands on their wives or the absolute power of the masters on their slaves. In general, it was more true that citizenship was more prevalent, as long as those given the right to vote were sufficiently wealthy and so did not tend to use their political power to rob the wealth.
>
> However, it was not possible for those who did not have enough time to understand political problems, who are mechanical and had a job, and who should have been at home, not on *the agora*, to be citizens. Citizenship was unlikely in Iran and the cold northern climates; because politics was impossible in these countries. It would make people super-hot, incapacitate despotism; extreme cold meant that people were contented to live a pure life. A state could not consist of many citizens; the meaning of many citizens was that the state ceased to be a state. More than ten thousand people could not know each other and make friendship".

Aristotle, who has the above thoughts, focused on the issue of assuming that the vital problem is the stable government in accordance with the law and that "people (men)" want to come to political positions in naturality. According to him, it was very important to find answers to questions about what kind of people should occupy political positions without an internal riot and uprising. For this, living in the police state was the "highest gift" for people according to Aristotle, and the intelligence of the good citizen was the highest human intelligence (Miller et al., 1995: 457). The understanding of citizenship that Aristotle represented here included the full acceptance of the classical or traditional understanding in Athens, and voiced the necessity to accept a "assuming a strict division" in society. In this understanding, while a definite distinction was accepted between the "public" and "home life", he saw the absolute "participation in decision-making" of the people who were accepted as citizens. This included an anti-democratic situation today and eliminated the distinction of "ruling and ruled". This situation is important in terms of revealing certain characteristics such as "being a known man, having a genealogy, being a warrior, and being a capitalist", which are necessary to become citizens in the Ancient Athens (Pocock, 1998). In addition to these general assumptions about the citizens in the police state, the participation of the citizens in the city life is one of the most natural processes of the Greeks. For this reason, "people" and "citizens" are used exactly in the Ancient Athens in the same sense. However, this does not mean that citizens do not have a "private space" as a social entity. At this point, it was accepted that the citizen in the Ancient Greek could have "individual freedom" as a person. However, in the political sense, this understanding is not taken to mean that a person may have a "special" personality, and again Aristotle was referred at this point. Aristotle, although evaluating the citizen through human beings, deemed it appropriate to evaluate as a "buried in society as part of a certain social whole" (Sartori, 1996: 308–309).

Considered in this context, the ideal of Aristotelian citizenship, which seems to be able to reach correct conclusions on the subject, gained a new content as a result of the emergence and development of Stoicism[1] during the Hellenistic Age and Roman Empire with the collapse of the Ancient Greek city states after Aristotle proposed these ideas. The idea

---

1 The basic teachings of the Stoa idea are a competently connected harmony between nature and a true moral system in general. According to them; a life in harmony with nature is to live in accordance with the will of the God. This is possible by cooperating with good powers, having a superhuman understanding that ensures being virtuous, and believing that the world is good and reasonable. Thus, a real harmony can be formed between human nature and general nature. In this sense, man appears in the Stoa as a rational being like the God. This situation gives people a special place in the world. Especially people have the ability to speak and to distinguish between good and bad; therefore, they can live social life, even social life is a necessity for man. According to them, human is evaluated by believing in fate. The social objectives of man are loyal to their values and that good people also get a share of it. At this point, people are a member of the "world state" according to the Stoa. Both gods and humans are the natural citizens of this state, and the constitution of this society is "mindwise that teaches people what to do and what not to do". This mind-wise is the nature law itself; it is the foundation of the being just and fair in every place. According to the Stoics, its principles are the same everywhere and always; it binds everyone. Even if s/he is a king, it doesn't matter. At this point, the law that exists for citizens is the power that dominates both gods and the behavior of all people. (A more detailed information on this subject, see Sabine, George H. (1965), **A History of Political Theory**, Holt, Rinehart and Winston INC., USA, Chapter VIII).

of Stoicism, which reached a more remarkable dimension in the works of Cicero (106–43 BC), is a view that advocates the legitimacy of the "right of people to manage their own rights", especially as long as citizens do not abuse it. The idea of Roman citizenship, which made this legitimate within the framework of the "Magistratibus Laws", found it appropriate for its citizens to live according to their own wishes, without being subject to a certain status, as long as they basically did not dispose of the freedom and preferences of others (Arena, 2016: 95). This is important in order to show that a more advanced understanding of citizenship was found in Rome according to the idea of the Ancient Greek and Aristotelian citizenship. It is clearly seen with the practices experienced that this is the understanding of citizenship inherited in the modern era by developing theoretically and historically in the West, especially starting from the Middle Ages.

Christianity, as an element that complements the Roman citizenship understanding, which seems to be a product of Stoic thought, came to the agenda in I and II centuries as a teaching[2] and a social phenomenon. With

---

2 Christianity, which emerges as a political and social structure through the Church institution, is the most important understanding of both political practice and political philosophy at the European level in terms of its entity as an authoritative and influential institution on the spiritual problems of people regardless of a state structure. The idea of Christianity preached the understanding that the world is shaped in accordance with the natural law and the destiny – not much different from the pagan Stoicism – the laws of the rulers should be justice, and that all people are equal in the eye of the God. Such ideas show that there are serious links between the Stoa and Christianity and that the effort to reconcile the law of the God and the law of nature took an important time of the "Church Fathers", who laid the foundations of Christian political and social philosophy. The teaching of Christianity is instilled that the Christians respect the established authority. Here, "the election" of the manager is highlighted. The doctrine of Christianity demands "respect for the rules of society". In this context, the view attributed to Aziz Polda is emphasized that the ruling power is a necessary result of human sinfulness. Christianity, emphasizing the obligation to respect the ruler at the beginning over this understanding, expresses that the ruler is "the messenger of the God", with the acceptance of the ruler's authority from the public. In this context, Christianity, according to his lawyers, has been the subject of evaluation by the people's choice is because of the reason for obedience to a divine leader, and "the power of the people to choose has shown the conforming of the power with the constitution, which are used in the broad sense". According to the idea of Christianity,

the fact that Christianity influenced the Western world epistemically and intellectually in the world, human beings were no longer delayed as "citizens of the whole world or the city of God". However, "citizenship of the earth" ceased to be or was an essential part of "good life" in this process (Miller et al., 1995). In this process, all the dogmas of Christianity were the main determinants in the political and social life and most importantly in the "justification" point. This lasted at least XI and XII centuries precisely, as generally accepted.

With the re-emergence of the idea of the Classical or Ancient reasoning, although the history of this could not be given clearly, the idea of pre-Christian citizenship in Europe was reappeared again in Europe at the end of the Middle Ages and with the Renaissance Europe. However, this was not in the context of the Greek city-state and formed from the Roman citizenship perspective and rose on the foundations of the Stoic thought (Miller et al., 1995: 457–458). Because in Rome, the vast majority of people were seen as an important argument for the continuation of the political structure with the emphasis on "society", which is the 'top sum' of human coexistence "for the vast majority of people" in the formation of citizenship. In this context, it was suggested that "a society based on mutual acquaintance *could be* mentioned" as a direct neighborhood relationship. Within this proximity that can be accepted from the cradle to the grave; each individual's place was seen in their local community. In this sense, the social structure is described in an official and informal dimension "within the jurisdiction of *marechaussée* (gendarmerie), which is an extraordinary event and a minor cause of concern, the first police force in the Western history and an organization composed of assembled detachments". This situation was later deemed important in the sense of the formation of an "identity" in the size of neighborhood relations on the scale of Europe, as a factor in the emergence of "duty" consciousness in society and more

---

"it was made a definite distinction between the authority attached to a theory, as one is theology and other is law, and the arbitrary power that an individual could have, so it was possible to coexist without breaking" (See a more extensive information on this subject; Sabine, George H. (1965), **A History of Political Theory**, Holt, Rinehart and Winston INC., USA, Chapters X).

importantly, as the basis of the formation of a social individual (Bauman, 2019: 27–28).

Citizenship, as a result of the vital and political environment of the Middle Ages, started to be reconsidered as a phenomenon dealt with in the context of the city and urbanization at the European level in this period. As the view on the idea that "urban atmosphere makes people free" for the period started to be discussed, the cities became areas where the feudal social structure formed on the basis of nobility and land owner-ship in the Middle Ages became "spaces where the transition towards free individuals was experienced". In these cities, the feudal structure began to be questioned, and the phenomenon of citizen or "*citoyen*", that is, "*urban people*", started to turn into "*individuals*" dealt within the framework of capitalist relations (Kadıoğlu, 2008b: 86).

At this point, it is seen that Magna Carta[3], which was accepted in 1215, came to the forefront in discussing the "individual" as a social and free

---

3 The text, which is "the Great Contract" in Turkish and whose real name is *Magna Carta Libertatum* (Convention of Freedoms), is a contract written in the medieval Latin language on a parchment sheet. This text has been specif-ically studied by anyone who has done research on political history, political thoughts, and law, and described as a world-famous "independence contract" that everyone, more or less, has knowledge today. The main subject of this text is the acceptance of a covenant, "stamped with the royal seal for the acquisition of individual rights and freedoms", which is regarded as a pioneer step in the West against the unlawful and unjust practices of the kingdom administrations in the Middle Ages within and above the feudal structure. Magna Carta, signed between British King John (Johannes) of the time, Pope III. Innocent (Innocentius), and the local rulers on June 15, 1215, was primarily intended to "solve the local and everyday problems in Britain of the period", while aiming to "impede the king's powers and emphasize that the law was more superior than the king". However, "its protest against violence against arbitrary gov-ernance", which was inherited from the 13th century, is seen as "a search for assurance for rights and freedoms" in the name of today. The text of which content is primarily dominated by the articles for ensuring the security of the church is a contract in which important decisions are taken for the solution of administrative problems between kings and feudal rulers. The Articles 39 and 40 of the text, in which "anxiety to balance" among the administrative powers are at the forefront, states that *"No free man shall be seized or imprisoned, or stripped of his rights or possessions, or outlawed or exiled, or deprived of his standing in any way, nor will we proceed with force against him, or send*

entity despite of many discussions. The nobility who tried to compel the British King John (John the Lackland/1166–1216) to grant them rights had already granted the similar rights, which they demanded from the King, to the community living in towns and cities with their own rulership. The nobles had demanded the rights, which were close to the rights they gave to society by Magna Carta in 1215, this time from the king. Although it has been presented as a contract in the name of the Western literature in terms of the development of individual and social citizens' rights and the gains of social freedom in many ways, Magna Carta has been subject to slightly different political and legal evaluations, according to some authors. In one of these, Magnus Ryan tried to explain Magna Carta, saying "In terms of legal logic (Magna Carta), it reveals something new, as it treats the kingdom not as a total of nationals but as a matter of rights. Just like the church and cities are treated as collective accepter of donations and privileges. Elsewhere, it took a large part of the 12th century that the town or city turns into a specific juridical zone, which forms a circle in which the ruling differences within it to be overridden by a regional and single legal order" (2011: 58–59). In this sense, during XI and XII centuries before Magna Carta, it has been observed that a remarkable social and political structure began to form in the Northern Italy. It was claimed that the development(s) experienced in this period was a departure from a feudal structure in social sense. Because, especially the urban structures strengthening and developing in the century underwent political and social transformations that would shake the thesis that "the monarchy that inherited from family is the only solid form of government". This paved the way for individuals and societies to establish some independent city republics, which are governed by "the will of the councils

---

others to do so, except by the lawful judgment of his equals or by the law of the land" (39) and "To no one will we sell, to no one deny or delay right or justice" (40) (Hindley, 1990). Here the text, known for leading the legal texts put forward within the framework of its own problems of many nations after itself, was compared with "The Sened-i İttifak" (The Charter of Alliance) that was made on September 29, 1808 between the Ottoman Grand Vizier Alemdar Mustafa Pasha and the leaders of the local people in Rumelia and Anatolia. (See Magna Carta for the whole and for more information; Hindley, Geoffrey (edit.-1990), **The Book of Magna Carta**, Constable & Robinson Ltd., London).

rather than the rulers" through the emphasis on "freedom". At this point, the city republics were able to form social and political structures that relatively provide freedom to the people of the region, through the consuls "that change almost every year". The first city with such political and social structures is Pisa in Italy, and it was founded in 1085. Then such a political system was adopted and implemented by the cities of Lombardy, Tuscany, Milan, Lucca, Bologna, and Siena. Again in the middles of the 12th century, the management of the councils in these cities evolved into a form of government where a civil servant called 'podesta' is centered in the political system and an elected government managed the work. The person in charge of this government was called "the highest power in the city" or "*potestas*". In this system, the officer called *podesta* had to be a citizen of another city; its reason is evaluated as "their local ties or loyalties do not disturb the impartiality of his administration over the judiciary". Only after this person was elected, he could gain the title of "representative of the people". This person also had the right to run the administration under the counseling of a council, the largest of which was made up of six hundred people, and a council normally limited to the city's forty citizens (Skinner, 2014: 23–24).

Citizenship functioning within the medieval Italian city states in this way under the framework of a political system started to be discussed in the "natural rights" dimension by such thinkers as William of Ockham (1285–1347) between XIII and XIV centuries according to an understanding of a ball of rights, especially in connection with the concept of "law of nature". In this regard, William's efforts are remarkable in the name of his era at the point of forming a citizenship theory. In this age, transforming the concept of '*dominium*' into "the concept of rights understood as the natural competence or the authority of action approved by 'law of nature'[4] or

---

4 Revealing legitimacy that can be accepted legally through human nature is an important problem area. The determination of this legitimacy is likely to be over "ethical" and "permanent natural legitimacy without prioritizing legal consequences". At this point, the phenomenon of "justice" came to the fore and included a process that formed the basis of "human rights" in modernity. In this sense, it is possible to form an "objectivist or subjectivist version according to an equality scheme like the rights arising from positive law rooted in the nature of things". The phenomenon of "equality" may be the cause of a moral

positive human law" was seen as an important problem area for William, and he put forward detailed ideas on this subject so. William, who tried to show that citizens do not get these rights because they are Christians, realized that the use of these rights is a necessity to be human. Because William, drawing attention to the entity of these rights prior to the birth of Jesus described "all the legal arrangements made by people, especially the judiciary (jobs), especially human activities concerning property and citizens". This idea was later seen as an effective point of view in the process of reforming the Aristotelian and church language to address citizenship "as a human imagination having rights related to a more specific benefit of human nature like a moral life in a political community in addition to natural rights such as self-protection and self-defense (benefits of animal nature)" (Brett, 2011: 119). Again in the 19th century, Dante (1265–1321) became the thinker who considered citizenship over "universal order" and "authority" within the framework of "hierarchical" relations on a social basis. Dante, considering the issue in Florence, evaluated citizenship through loyalty to the Empire as the secular authority instead of loyalty to religious authority, and he described citizens as entities having rights and

---

and legal confusion here, and at another point, it also gives the opportunity to develop for the facts within the whole of its necessity. However, at the point where the concept of equality exists under "nature", it is not always possible to solve the problem between the individual's "dignity" and "non-transferable". In this context, there are different interpretations regarding the concepts of "nature of things" and "human nature" at the fore point. Accordingly, it is believed that natural law in the past and today and the concept of "natural law" related to it, contributed to bring human nature to the forefront in a "historical-comparative" understanding in an individual, social and political common basis. In this context, three points can be brought to the fore in order to verify the natural law approach; "1) primarily the realism of the nature of things, namely a classic natural law that imposes itself; 2) but this realism has spread to human nature and in a very short time it has had to compromise with idealism that invaded this nature, namely modern pure naturalism; 3) and finally the realism of the nature of man, which is real "personalism" in natural law, has reappeared; and when human nature or natural law comes to the fore, it should be noted that, it is always under dual view (legal and political)" (Trigeaud, 2003: 384–385).

responsibilities constituted through the feeling of "patriotism" to political authority (Pocock, 1975: 50).

In the 17th century, many administrative procedures, including legal records, were revised in the framework of the Roman Law in some cities such as Nuremberg. This work was accepted as the first attempt to renew the cities themselves legally in a broad manner. New cities established in this way were promising personal freedom and providing everyone staying there for more than a year, the right to join the legal community of the city residents (*burgher*). Here, in this legal text, it was used the expression of *"whoever stays in this city for one year and one day without being asked to be returned by anyone, they will be protected against others and crowned with their freedom."* With this text, the emergence of the first facts, which included a serious guarantee at the point of responsibility of the city within the scope of legal assurance for citizens, started to become apparent in this way (Höfert, 2011: 78).

When these examples are analyzed, it is seen that a type of citizenship having started to be considered as an entity to gain individual and legal rights, has begun to be discussed legally, politically, and socially. Here, the important Italian philosopher Machiavelli (1469–1527) attributed the dignity of the citizen to the *"virtue"*[5] of the citizens in Rome's magnificent

---

5 In the sense of emphasizing virtue in the philosophical point, the concept, used as a "permanent position in the stable implementation of moral virtues", is to "emphasize the political one" in the literature, by using the concept of virtue over Montesquieu, Voltaire, and Kant, which are generally thinkers of Enlightenment, in the sense of "preference that is deemed appropriate for general interest rather than private interest". The concept is thought to be inherited to Machiavelli and the Enlightenment thinkers over "courage" with the emphasis on "human" in the Roman period historically and theoretically based on *"virtu"* and Cicero's *"vertu"* without including for 'woman'. Especially through the phenomenon of *"fortitudo moralis"*, Kant strengthened his understanding that "the courage becomes virtue when an opponent confronts our moral purpose", which emphasizes that the purpose of human virtue is the happiness of others by human becomes perfect (see more for a detailed information; Labarriére, Jean-Louis (2003), "Erdem (Virtue)", Trans. İsmail Yerguz, **Siyaset Felsefesi Sözlüğü**, Edit. Philippe Raynaud-Stéphane Rials, İletişim Yayınları, Istanbul, ss. 305–312). Citizenship virtue is also referred to as "civic virtue" in the literature and can be translated into Turkish as a "common good" in line with the politically defined virtue understanding and attracted attention as a

period and found it appropriate to draw a citizen portrait based on this meaning. In his times, Machiavelli, who compared the powerful stand and stable structure of the Ancient Roma and the defeated situation of the city of Florence of which he was a member by his enemies easily, due to the instability he experienced, tried to explain that reason with that the Roman citizens had virtue. Because, according to Machiavelli, citizen's virtue is a situation related to *"...self-discipline, patriotism, slavishness, and willingness to give up personal gains for the sake of public benefit"* (Miller et al., 1995: 457–458). This situation, for Machiavelli, is abundant in the Romans. The views put forward by Machiavelli on this subject were elaborated in his work, especially on *"Discourses on the First Decade of Titus Livius"*.[6]

Machiavelli, who discusses what might happen if the citizen virtue disappears from time to time on the basis of the city of Florence and on the example of the Ancient Rome, felt the need to explain the dangers faced by the "freedom of the city" through some tensions that occurred

---

fact that is included in the discussions of republicanism. This understanding is a phenomenon that is handled within the "social negotiation" processes within the "humanism" understanding of the Renaissance period instead of the Christian based solidarity. It is an understanding that puts the individual and the society at the center of the idea of "common-interest" with the emphasis on "the being public" in line with the purpose of reaching the common good of citizens, especially within the framework of the republican tradition. In this way, while an important argument is provided for individuals in the society to understand each other, it is seen as an expected benefit with this understanding that individuals respect each other's rights in cultural and political ways (see more for a detailed information on this issue; Dagger, Richard (1997), **Civic Virtues, Rights, Citizenship and Republican Liberalism**, Oxford University Press, Oxford).

6   In Machiavelli's book, which was with its original name called *"Discourses on the First Decade of Titus Livius"* and known its date written as 1513–1517, his political views that put him at the center of modern political thought and his ideas of the republic over the ancient Rome were clearly revealed. This is the work by which Machiavelli produced his detailed ideas on citizenship, revealing his views in modern political thought that paved the way for the discussion of the citizen phenomenon on a public and social basis (see; Mavhiavelli, Niccolo (1998), **Discourses on Livy**, Translated by Harvey C. Mansfield and Nathan Tarcov, The University of Chicago Press, Chicago & London).

on a social basis in the city in the 13th century. According to Machiavelli; when the Aristocrats ruled in Florence in the 1340s, the people "witnessed that the majesty of their administration was destroyed, the traditions were abolished, and their rights were cancelled", when a duke turned him into a tyrant. For this reason, the people opposed tyrants as a result of a natural right and managed to establish their own regime after a struggle that continued for a while. However, since the people, who were described as "unbridgeable crowds" by Machiavelli, took full sovereignty and control of the regime, the regime first became corrupt and then "turned into an extreme freedom". After when the balance of power was once again in favor of the aristocrats, the freedoms of the people were weakened again, and the process leading to a new bully rule occurred spontaneously. This situation can be explained in two ways for Machiavelli: "to provide different citizens with favor, to protect them from state officials, to help them money, to achieve the ranks they do not deserve, to provide a false-popularity for the public with various games and public awards, and to organize expensive demonstrations calculated to bluff their way through losing their freedom" (Skinner, 2004: 121–122). In both cases, the weakening of the people emerges as a rule especially for the city states and becomes the main reason for the people to lose constantly and to weak their rights in the system. When it is read through the views of Machiavelli as a concept and fact, it is seen that citizenship has been inherited by the modern era as one of the general dilemmas of "freedom" and "virtue".

Considering the principles of virtue/loyalty/freedom at this point and evaluated in connection with Machiavelli's thoughts with more positive references, the declaration of "the Commonwealth[7] and the Free State" in

---

7 The management established at the end of the rebellion movement carried out on the adversary of the monarchy, which started in the Netherlands first and then in England in 1649 on the separations of religion and resulted in the execution of King Charles I under the influence of the Republican thought and the republican citizenship related to it and with the effect of ideas developed by Machiavelli. The Commonwealth (Republic), also known as the Cromwell's Government and declared by the parliament under its leadership, also referred to as the Army Commander Oliver Cromwell (1599–1658), which was historically the leader of the rebellion, lasted from 1649 to 1658. This situation made itself felt philosophically as a "republicanism" movement in England for a while over some

England in 1649, one century after his death, is important for the recognition and identification of citizenship. With this regime trial in England, the demand of citizenship became the basis for raising wider concerns over "freedom". This concern came to the forefront that freedom can only be sustainable if being a community's member. It was possible to be the subject of discussion in England of the Commonwealth period that the guarantee of freedom can be possible by being a member of a community rather than an individual with an advanced understanding according to its period. So, the citizen's freedom could be discussed again in an "urban" and "national" dimensions, and concrete demands on the rights of citizens in the name of the modern era first reached the point of finding response (Gordon & Stack, 2007: 123). An important result of these developments is the evaluation of citizenship through "settling in a free state", which can be considered in this context and also emerged as "New-Romanian theory"[8].

British thinkers. By this initiative thought to lay the groundwork for modern republicanism, which is reconsidered over the rights of citizens, it is included in the "mixed regime" of Commonwealth, such as "highlighting civil virtue, protecting the independence of armed citizens, glorifying the non-personal law accepted as the guarantee of freedom". It is thought that Commonwealth contributed to the filling of the content of the important rights and freedoms for ordinary citizens in the "mixed regime" such as "the prominence of civil virtue, the protection of independence of armed citizens, the glorification of non-personal law accepted as the guarantee of freedom" (Audier, 2006: 31).

8 The thought evaluated around the "Roman Antiquity" in some discussions was handled by Hegel in the modern period. According to Hegel, throwing moral individuals into the fire is also to make all gods and souls an abstract generality. For this reason, in the universal sovereign pantheon, the conditions in which individuality will yield are not resisted. According to Hegel, this is "restarting a classical discussion on Rome in the national growth plane of individuals". This led to the exaltation of the Roman great personalities in Europe, and considered as the inability to overcome the civilization virtue of Rome during the republican period. However, this point of view ignored the decline of the understanding of freedom and equality during the imperial period of Rome. Besides, a great deal of archive information was lost during the Imperial and division periods of Rome. For this reason, it is difficult to obtain exact information about this period of Rome. Especially after the Renaissance, it was seen that the Roma and the Roman myths produced heroic examples that contrast traditions and historical social reality. During this period, such topics were discussed with the Stoa ideal, which the Roman Republic thinkers, Polybios and Cicero regarded

Citizens' rights found wide scope in the UK with columns and articles published on some newspapers of that day. These debates were carried out largely by "classical ideas on freedom" by John Milton (1608–1674), who was a principal republican thinker of the time and secretary of the state council of the Commonwealth. As a result of these efforts, important steps took to establish/place a citizenship understanding within the framework of a full-scale republican theory. Within the framework of this understanding, during the fall of the Commonwealth and the restoration of the monarchy in Britain, it was connected with "the perception of modern civil society as a moral space between the rulers and the ruled… and with such institutions like the labor market" by Henry Neville (1620–1694) and Algernon Sidney (1623–1683). Though the Commonwealth cannot be maintained as a regime, civil rights became an irreversible area of discussion intellectually in the state structure. This idea was tried to be explained by "the relationship between freedom of nationality and the powers of the state" and it was evaluated that it could be developed at the point of "it can be kept with an unlimited use of a series of specific civil rights" (Skinner, 2017: 36–39). These developments definitely paved the way for the recognition of citizens' rights at the "freedom" point in specific to England.

At this point, the developments in England are important for recalling that the concept of "citizenship duty" was brought to the agenda on behalf of the citizen by classical republican writers, especially in parallel with economic and social rights in addition to freedom. According to the classic republican writers, many of whom are mentioned above, it is also an important problem to prevent the government acting on behalf of its

---

as mysterious and addressed it within the framework of "politicization of special virtues". In this context, the superiority of citizens' rights and responsibilities over the Roman public law was discussed as compared to previous and subsequent civilizations. This superiority is explained by the understanding of the "mixed constitution" that emphasizes the social "balance" and by "the stability" of a republic regime. In this way, Rome was shown as an exemplary political system for modern societies (For a detailed information on this topic, see: Lecoq, Jean-François (2003), "Roma Antikitesi (Roman Antiquity)", Trans. İsmail Yerguz, **Siyaset Felsefesi Sözlüğü**, Edit. Philippe Raynaud-Stéphane Rials, İletişim Yayınları, İstanbul, ss. 717–724).

own community from preventing the danger of falling into the hands of passionate or self-interested individuals. The approach proposed in this context, "the protection of a free life style should support the political processes of all citizens and the participation is for these processes" is described as an important stage of the balance of right and duty in the name of citizenship (Skinner, 2006: 182–183). The balance of rights and duties on behalf of citizenship is still an area of debate over its dimensions and limitations throughout the modern period.

Particularly the discussions at this point continued within the framework of the above developments for three centuries after Machiavelli. In most parts of the Western geography, primarily in England, the phenomenon was evaluated over such thinkers as Thomas Hobbes (1588–1679), John Locke (1632–1704), Bernard Mandeville (1670–1733), JJ Rousseau (1712–1778), and Benjamin Constant (1767–1830). Citizenship was handled in this process from ideal to practical, and the concept was started to be discussed through "individual freedom" and the apparatus of "modern state" that was reshaped through the French Revolution (Miller et al., 1995: 459):

> "(In the 18th century), the state institutions (first palace, then government and bureaucracy) became increasingly public; it was formal, different, and relatively open. The laws of the state should now be officially announced and published, and printed in a language that the public would understand, and distributed everywhere in a language that the public would understand. In many countries, both military and civil servants of the state started to wear uniforms to emphasize the difference and integrity of the state apparatus.
>
> Thus, the state had transformed into a different level of political functions and officials, moving away from the society. At the same time, the state had the power to affect the whole society with its activities. When looked at the place where the state is located, the society consisted of a large number of *particuliers* and pure individuals, sometimes privileged. The state was approaching these individuals who would pay their taxes and recruited etc., but thought that they were not qualified to take active roles in state affairs (Poggi, 1991: 83)".

This situation separates the state and society from each other in the modern world. However, it ensures that freedom, which is the privilege of a group of minorities on behalf of citizens in the ancient world, is developed as "general human freedom". Until one century ago, there was not even any debate on these developments at this point, except for England.

Considering this case; it is seen that an important and rapid process start in the name of citizen rights and responsibilities. In England, Hobbes is at the forefront at this point. It is seen that Hobbes started to clarify the position of the individual while strengthening legitimacy of the state through rights and responsibilities. However, the general aim in Hobbes is to ensure the sovereignty of the state. That is; Hobbes clarifies the issue of sovereignty over individual power and the power of the owner of this sovereignty. Here, Hobbes tries to explain clearly what the disobedience of the individual may cost. According to Hobbes, "... reasonable people could understand that they had to hand on the sovereign as much power as needed to prevent this destruction without the need for further discussion ...". Hobbes, who wants to clarify this issue further, explains the subject through the "state of nature". Hobbes stated that the individual tries to find the self-protection mechanism by using his "mind". Although Hobbes' perspective is seen as a problematic understanding for the conceptualization of the state, it is a determination to be seen as a definition of legitimacy after a while (Carnoy, 2014: 34–35). This determination of Hobbes ensured that the issue was constantly kept on the agenda later and that the rights and responsibilities of the citizens were a matter of debate, first in England and then in the whole West.

This type of discussion spread to the rest of Europe over the "general human freedom" by the 18th century. Although this understanding is not known in all aspects in the Western thought, it became a search for a political and social model. The subject, along with the developments in the Colonial America, had an important place on the basis of developments regarding freedom (Hayek, 2008: 46).

While these developments were taking place in the Anglo-Saxon world, "Patriotic Citizenship Culture" started to form in France, following the Seven Years' War, in the early years according to the French Revolution. It is claimed that this culture is not a result of the French Revolution but one of its reasons and it is a "formed" phenomenon that covers the whole 21st century. One of the advocates of this view, Schama found that patriotic citizenship was a result of the dynamic aspects of pre-revolutionary France as well, arguing that "...the French Revolution is more a random and chaotic event, a product of human mediation rather than structural conditioning". Schama, emphasizing the relationship between "patriotism and freedom"

(2015: 11), opened a different perspective to the modern period development of citizenship. The following views of Bauman that reveals the accuracy of Schama's above views to some extent on the meaning of freedom in
the modern period and regarding the discussion of the relationship between
these two concepts in different ways in the Western world are important:

> "Libraries of books have been written on the uniqueness of the modern
> (Western) phenomenon and its many remarkable qualities. But sociologically,
> two of the many unique features of modern freedom undoubtedly deserve spe-
> cial attention: its close relationship with individuality and the hereditary and
> cultural connection with market economy and capitalism...
>   ...We can add that this eccentricity is not a cultural perception that attributes
> a special value (special opportunities, special duties, special moral duties etc.)
> to a single man, separate from the group to which he belongs. Perceptions of
> this kind can be found in many cultures long before the fact that the so-called
> "Western man" appeared in its well-known form, (but)... as long as it is a real
> individual (i.e. a free selector, an independent carrier of moral responsibility, a
> master of his own life), he is placed outside the ordinary, everyday life, paying
> the price for human freedom by waiving social duties and leaving behind the
> haughty flurry of worldly matters; (in this context)... the individuality of the
> modern inner world, tied to the original, modern form of freedom, can be
> stated as a universal character of people, and moreover, as the most determi-
> nant among the most universal or universal qualities, and it has been as well
> (2018: 53–54)".

It is seen that Bauman tried to depict freedom in the modern period with
its cultural dimension as well as originality and universal qualities in the
theoretical framework above. The attempts were made in France, where
the modern citizenship concept, which was the subject of debate over the
concept of freedom, was handled as "a concept that includes everyone
without excluding any members of a society". With "The Declaration
of the Rights of Man and of the Citizen", published in 1789, and "The
French Constitution", come into force in 1791, it can be clearly seen the
basic ideas regarding modern human rights. In these texts, the new content of the phenomenon of citizenship emerged as a different thought,
bringing the "idea of basic equality" to the agenda for the first time in the
modern sense. According to Ayse Buğra, it is that the concept of "rightness", which forms the basis of justice, is replaced by equal rights in the
context of the modern citizenship relationship. While rightness defines who
should behave to whom and how based on their social status, the idea of

basic equality determines the relationships among the right-holder citizens (2008: 159). In "The Declaration of the Rights of Man and of the Citizen", especially the aristocracy in the country was targeted, and it was strongly emphasized that the initiative is not in the king and the aristocracy but in the concept of "law" for the use of political power. In a text that can be accepted as the founding law of a country, it is an important development to address the "rule of law" concept in a concrete manner. In particular, the absolute idea in this declaration is that "nobody has privileges or be subjected to discrimination due to their inherent characteristics" (Beriş, 2016: 659). Despite the fact that the declaration had such clear thoughts and was the founding text of the country in a political and constitutional way, the developments in France during the Revolution process showed that it is practically impossible to form a mentality linked to this text. The developments regarding regime change in the country were experienced at a dizzying pace. In particular, what happened in order to reach freedom immediately caused great traumas in the political and social point. It is observed that "the results of a social-revolutionary crisis and a centralized and bureaucratic state organization emerged in the country, which proved that it was impossible to stabilize" rather than what was done to ensure the "rule of law" on behalf of citizens in the country (Skocpol, 2004: 329).

The developments related to citizenship that can be considered relatively contradictory throughout the French Revolution are the most efficient source that strictly nourishes the rhetorical and theoretically citizenship concept based "equality" during the modern period. It is important that John Rawls, two centuries after the French Constitution of 1791, regarded the two fundamental principles highlighted in this text in terms of the meaning of rightness among individuals in society especially in this regard and expressed their provision still as a priority today:

> "1. Each person has an equal right in a system where equal fundamental freedoms are fully provided for all, in harmony with a system where freedom is provided for all.
> 2. Social and economic inequalities have to fulfill two conditions; a) first of all, they should be linked to public functions and positions within the conditions of fair equality of opportunity; b) should provide the most benefit to the members of society living in the most unfavorable conditions (Rawls, 2006: 145)".

Especially, "Declaration of the Rights of Man and of the Citizen" published in 1789 is important in terms of reflecting a holistic view of equality in the Western literature. The declaration, due to the emphasis that "any principle of sovereignty is national", remains the most important text that enables the discussion of citizenship in a dimension including freedom. Because the declaration at this point, with the guidance of the principle of "separation of powers" of Montesquieu (1689–1755), tried to determine the clear place of the forces forming the state to ensure freedom (Troper, 2011: 346). The declaration took the first steps towards the solution of many citizenship problems, including equality, within the framework of "public law" and "constitutional law" towards the end of the 13th century. According to Schama, this state of the declaration states that the French Revolution "gave birth to a new type of political world" at this point. It is also an important reality that "this world goes between two irreconcilable interests – establishing a strong state and forming a community of free citizens" – that passes to the present day. Here, for Schama, the emergence of legal norms on behalf of the citizen should be considered in the sense that "everyone can take their right without harming anyone else and that this impossibility is realized as an effort to reconstruct the history" (2015: 28). While this occasionally manifests itself in the desire of the French Revolutionaries to achieve "the best political order", it also manifested itself in the idea of total rejection of the existing social orders within the framework of the word "progress". In this context, a step has been taken historically to "overcome the actions by rejecting its meaning even if it is not the entity of universal measures". The French Revolution, together with the influence of the French radicalism, is an important factor in the foundation of the acceptance of modern society in the basis that people can live comfortably in this world as in their own home (Strauss, 2011: 35).

The emergence of the phenomenon of "public sovereignty" rhetorically and theoretically during the days of the French Revolution is also an important factor in the transformation of social imagination and the formation of a modern society, which is considered as a community of citizens. The phenomenon of popular sovereignty was put forward as a theory in those days. The phenomenon penetrated into social thoughts after a while and caused the thoughts that centered on the society to transform within the framework of their theoretical and practical meanings. The development process of the phenomenon followed two paths according to theorists. According to the first theory, based on the understanding of the contract, it developed in a dimension that "shapes the imagination of the groups that adopts these practices". According to the second theory, it is "reinterpretation of an application already existing in the old administration". The emphasis here is that legitimacy approaches used to be dominant in the past have taken place in the new order again. For this reason, the phenomenon transformed without any obvious interruption and made itself accept. However, in the acceptance of popular sovereignty in the Western literature, it is possible to explain the establishment conditions of the USA in those days. In the United States, the phenomenon has been seen as "… the idea of establishment that mythical old times would be drawn out and as something that people could do today ". According to this view, the establishment of a society is an action that can occur as a result of collective action in a completely secular world. Already this process, with all its practices, manifested itself in the chain of events that took place throughout the 18th century (Taylor, 2006: 112–113). As a result of these chain events, even if we limit them to the Western societies, the dimension of popular sovereignty can be explained as follows according to Albrecth Wellmer:

> "(Members of the Western societies) … are the people who have civil rights, regardless of the criteria for the recognition of rights. The choice of such a reference point includes the need to separate citizen rights from human rights. The "hegemon people" of such societies is the embodiment of all people equipped with citizenship rights. As for other people, they are implicitly considered members of another "hegemon people" and at least theoretically, more or less neglected. In other words, the societies that I have chosen as the reference point in the first stage of my explanations are the societies that are unsociable and of which borders are clearly defined against outside, at the political and moral level. Naturalness is here mentioned as a political-moral fixation (2006: 307)".

Citizenship provides its practical development through the notion of public sovereignty, which was observed to be dealt with depending on the developments in the French Revolution and the American War of Independence in the 18th century. When citizenship is taken up through the idea of "equality" in this period, it can be discussed particularly with the developments in the inner planes of the societies. Based on the entire

European plane; the basis of the modern citizenship phenomenon can be based on the concept of "civil rights" that began to be used in the courts in the centuries of the XVII and XVIII centuries. However, the development of parliamentary political systems in the West in the 19th century and the start of discussion of "political rights" is a turning point in the equality debates on citizenship. In the discussion of these rights, it is an example of what happened in England at the social and economic point. It is not a coincidence that these developments and debates started on the basis of the UK. Because the driving force of the West in terms of urbanization, industrialization, and economic development has been England during the modern periods. For these reasons, the living standards, the legal processes based on employment, and the social transformations that occurred in the UK during the 19th century are parallel to each other. For Karl Polanyi, the example of UK is important for the establishment of universal standards that strengthen "inequality" in terms of the minimum requirements of individuals but for "rights"-oriented developments after him:

> "In England, both land and money were organized before labor. Since the laborer was actually limited by the jurisdiction of the church to which he was affiliated, he prevented the formation of a national labor market by strict laws that prevent displacement. The Act of Settlement (1662), which set the rules for the situation called the 'parish serfdom', was loosened in 1795... the Speenhamland Act or Allowance System that was released this year... was in the direction of strengthening the paternalist labor order. According to this law, in the case of a loaf of bread is 1 shill, every poor and laborer takes 3 shillings a week for livelihood; 6 shillings and 1 penny for the livelihood of his wife and other family members. This will be provided either by his or his family's labor or by tax revenues for this purpose... These figures varied by region, but the Speenhamland criterion had been adopted in many places. This was considered a state of emergency measure and was accepted informal. Although it is often referred to as law, the measure itself was never enacted. But soon it became a local law in most of the rural areas, and even later in some industrial areas. It was a social and economic discovery that could actually be called a 'right to life' and prevented the formation of a competitive labor market until its abolition in 1834 (2006: 126–127)".

While these developments are taking place in the rights of the citizen in England, the restriction of the president's powers and the acquisition of powers of the Congress' financial and administrative control of the federal administrative apparatus on behalf of the society in the United States are important developments seen throughout the 19th century. It is seen that politicians who need the support of citizens to succeed in the presidential and congressional elections in the United States in this period started to use some ways to get votes from voters. Politicians struggled to overcome the concerns of citizens that people coming to rule "would seize power forever". For this purpose, some detailed arrangements were made on that the same person may be present at the Congress for a certain period of time, regarding the situation of coming to power by election. These rules had been introduced into the United States Constitution in the 1820s already. This situation was later adopted as a principle in democratic states, especially the Western democracies, at the point of development of liberal representative democracy. These developments were accepted as "everyone has equal rights in owing administrative duties and refusal to establish monopoly on duties", and it provided the establishment of understanding that "democracy is fed by equality: equality finds expression about voting (and)... ensures that everyone takes part in public administration at the same time" (Dreyfus, 2007: 154–155).

In this way, the legal developments in England and the transformations that took place in the United States within the framework of constitutional and political rights are of structural importance in terms of the acceptance of citizens' rights by the states. Based on these developments, the "welfare state"[9] system developed in the Western states with the 19th

---

9 This term has been produced to mean a situation in which citizens are generally involved in housing, education, and social services, but at the point where they can benefit from the income and health services necessary for their minimum living. In this context, it is important to state the role of the state in providing welfare services and privileges for its citizens. Especially, significant developed states have found themselves gradually in the face of increasing urbanization and population at the point of industrialization since the end of the 19th century. The "national insurance system" provided to citizens on health is the leading state initiative in this regard. This system, which was put into effect in Germany in 1884, was later adopted by the other European and Western states and transformed into a larger-scale situation with the payment of "pension (retired)" provided by employee cuts. However, family benefits, sickness, unemployment, and old-age insurance were accepted as important reforms in this regard in the 1930s and 1940s, especially in the United States. At this point, the term "Keynesian welfare state" has been put forward, and the phenomenon has

century. In this system, "social rights", an important discussion area for citizenship, started to occupy the agenda (Kadıoğlu, 2008b: 86). It is an unquestionable case today that the understanding of the welfare state was rapidly accepted in the Western democracies since the second half of the 20th century. The welfare state was strongly supported by citizens of the Western states. Large masses made significant gains in benefiting from the institutional structures of the welfare state and the growing wealth of their country. According to some authors, the welfare state emerged "government protected income, nutrition, health, housing, and minimum standards of education are provided citizens not as a donation but as a political donation". In this structure, specialized social service elements, guaranteed and supported by governments, are in the basic position. Thus, the level of welfare that the welfare state is trying to produce constituted an important reason for the continuation of the welfare society (Berting, 2017: 154–155). The welfare state, along with many transformations, has been a structural system that has been carried out structurally by the countries of continental Europe until today. It is still a political system trying to maintain its entity as an important modern state understanding.

The welfare state, considering the adventure above, has been the subject of debate over the phenomenon of "positive rights" that offers to the public generally. Because positive rights have been assessed through two different understandings that put different missions on the welfare state in the West. In this context, positive rights are handled within the framework of the citizen understanding, which is considered to be "innate liberal" in the United States, and the citizen in this discourse is defined as either "possessing all power (libertarians) or having no power (communitarians)". In Europe, the

---

experienced transformations including different meanings by many ideological and political understandings of state. However, many debates continue today whether this situation corrects the situation of gender equality and "equality" between social groups. In the face of developments such as "economic stagnation" and "unemployment rates", it is seen as an important problem area within the framework of the phenomenon of "populism", which continues on whether the state should be citizen-oriented or state-oriented. (See more a detailed information, Williams, Fiona (2016), "Refah Devleti (Welfare State)", Trans. Ahmet Kemal Bayram, **Sosyal Bilimler Ansiklopedisi 'İkinci Kitap/L-Z'**, Edit. Adam Kuper-Jessica Kuper, Adres Yayınları, Ankara, pp. 1154–1157).

citizen is defined as "not dominating or dominated, but as possessing different degrees of power". In this sense, the phenomenon of "civil society" has been brought to the fore in the name of citizenship. Addressing two different positive rights conceptions in the West has also identified different perspectives in seeking answers to questions on how civil society will function and how government and civil society conceptions will occur. The main reason for these differences is the historical processes that the two understandings have experienced. Given as an example; the power of the citizen in Britain was conceived in a way related to social, economic, and birth, and in France as a political and intellectual entity that acquired power by will. These differences are also closely related to "nation-state formation processes". The most important fact that clearly shows us the historical development difference between the Western Europe and the United States is the establishment conditions of the nation-state (Strath, 2011: 215).

"Citizenship" is an important separation point in discussions about how the adventure in the West is maintained in the nation-state formation. The difference between Europe and the United States appears to be stronger, especially in cases where democracy comes before the bureaucracy, and where civil and legal rights prevail over social rights. The phenomenon of "social citizenship" existing in the United States constitutes a paradox for the country to be defined in the context of this issue in the face of political systems in Europe. In the United States, citizens' relations with the state can be partly determined within the framework of the contractual arrangements they have made with the state and the things what they receive as help from the state. The citizen is the main actor in the state system in Europe. This is important in terms of revealing the differences of the Western states' view of citizens in the evaluation of the welfare state in the nation-states dimension (Kadıoğlu, 2009). Despite the different perspectives of nation-states in the West, the fact that citizens are the most basic actors of politics in the welfare state stands before us as an important situation.

The most important situation appeared by the process in the point of view of the changes in the viewpoint of citizens in the modern period is the belief that the differences between the countries having the understanding of the welfare state can be overcome within the framework of the "liberal and social democratic consensus" on behalf of the Western states. This may include some critical points of view as in the above paragraph. However, it has been evaluated as a contribution to the transformation of different political and intellectual movements in England, France, and the United States into the understandings that give the same result in different ways (Bellamy, 1992). In addition, the fact that citizenship is the product of a common understanding for the sustainability of modern life in the Western states has enabled citizenship to be considered as a social "educational project". Especially in citizenship education, "handling personally responsible and participatory citizenship within the framework of 'political' concepts" is a general acceptance that shows that a common goal is aimed. It is the result of an education that is universally based on citizens and an understanding of "justice" based on pedagogically "equality" (Weinberg & Flinders, 2018: 583–584).

The emergence of the "state of law" and the conditions of its emergence, which are tried to be established in the West as educational and experiential, are important for sustaining the gains of citizenship. At the point of equality, justice, and human rights, the main line of development of the state is closely related to the development of the rule of law in Europe. Most widely, the state of law has been defined as "the compliance of people with the law and the rule of law..." When this definition is taken in a way that includes the citizen, that is the state of law that is tried to be theorized politically and legally, it means "the state is subject to law and governed by law". In this respect, the state of law is considered as "administration by law, not by people" (Raz, 2008: 151). Although this is described as quite "general and abstract", the state of law is an important phenomenon in the development process of the philosophical and practical point of the understanding of citizenship developing in the dimension of rights. Because this understanding has provided at least theatrically a general acceptance of universal law, which is tried to be processed through the "principle of causality" in the West, instead of a private law based on the individual.

Throughout the 20th century, it has been observed that the most important discussion area that developed in the name of citizenship on whether through the notions of the welfare state or the rule of law has been concentrated within the framework of "political equality" as the most important discussion area of the subject. As the 20th century starts, it is accepted that only forty-eight states in the world are considered to be completely independent, and the number of those that can only be regarded as "representative democracy" in the nearest sense to date is eight. It is known that only one of these eight countries (New Zealand) has basic democracy institutions and women have the right to vote. The statistical situation is that there is a serious problem in the world about whether it is possible to talk about a political equality among citizens in the world in a very short time before today. However, throughout the first quarter of the 20th century, Great Britain stands out as the healthiest representation of democracy in the world. Here, it is seen that the working class and then the women were able to gain their rights at the point of political equality. The development of citizens in political equality in Great Britain is very fast and positive in terms of being able to participate and be elected in the House of Commons elections, as well as being elected to the Cabinet or even the Prime Minister. The importance of these developments in England in terms of obtaining political rights of other citizens around the world is a serious development considering that right to elect and be elected of African-American citizens in the United States can only be achieved through *Voting Rights*, which came into force in 1965 (Dahl, 2018: 31). As can be seen; on the basis of the 19th century, it is seen that the citizenship debate can be addressed on practices that can be considered quite new when it comes to political equality.

One of the most important developments for the gains of citizenship in terms of political equality is the reconciliation of central governments and liberalism with regard to the economic system in a process involving the entire 20th century. This situation has been handled differently from the modern period to the post-modern period and subject to different analyzes in the discussions on behalf of citizenship. The issue of the economic system has paved the way for ideological debates that affect the equality among citizens, positively for some and negatively for others, by the post-modern period. According to Michael Sandel, who has a negative view of this consensus, the developments experienced are not a manifestation of moral attitude. For Sandel, it is criticized that the complex problems and troubles of the modern industrial order have been brought to the fore in terms of "public interest in principle" against democracy through the phenomenon of nation. Because Sandel stated that it was wrong to focus on the construction of the state as a modern economic device of which sole purpose is "to shape the common life", instead of the idea of a "virtuous republic" based on democracy during the 20th century (2006). Citizenship, which the state apparatus developing within the framework of this understanding, has been theorized from a politically liberal perspective for a long time as "a formal and principally universal legal status protecting individuals firstly". Citizenship, when looking at the republicanism dimension in addition to this theory, is described as an entity formed as "a collective self-management possibility that realizes the freedom and other common goods that the individual cannot achieve alone". The main argument here is that freedom cannot be achieved naturally. It is emphasized that the construction of a "legal status" based on "civil virtue" can only be valuable for freedom through an active understanding of citizenship (Honohan, 2017: 2). When evaluated through this binary context, the position of the citizen in the modern period depends on the reconciliation of the state with the individual politically and economically. In this way, the emergence of human being as a product, whose responsibilities are permanent and whose worries on "freedom" and "equality" are removed, is still an unresolved situation as a paradoxical situation.

Considering the change, transformation and achievement above, it is observed that the modern citizenship concept has been theoretically "hybridized" in a mixed way. In this process, citizenship has made a certain step in line with the development and transformation of the liberal economy, but with the notion of "state of law" through the discussions of political equality. Today, however, citizenship have not still resolved the uncertainty of the individual in terms of what the individual politically is and will be. Especially in the "post-modern period", it is not possible to solve these issues or at least a positive solution for the position and situation of the citizen. According to Andrew Heywood, who has an analysis of the political concepts and phenomena experienced and formed in the modern period, it is seen that the views on the citizenship debates in the modern period have become more complicated. According to Heywood, the citizenship relationship is "a relationship between the individual and the state". In this relationship, "(individual and state) are linked by mutual rights and duties. Citizens are different from nationals and foreigners because they are full members of their political community or state based on ownership of fundamental rights". In this context, citizenship according to Heywood is a phenomenon "that can be evaluated in different ways depending on whether it is shaped by individualism or collectivism/communitarianism" (2012: 211).

As can be seen; in the post-modern period it has become more difficult in intellectual, political, social, and legal meanings to explain the situation of citizenship in theoretical terms against the state or its structures, which can be considered instead of it. Here, it is important to be read it through the community or other political structures as well as an emphasis on the state. Because the evaluations made in order to determine the belonging of the citizen both conceptually and theoretically and also the confusion in the discussions on this issue introduce a problem area.

II Citizen as an Aware Entity in the Modern Period

Citizenship is a phenomenon taking many different forms while defining the individual politically, socially, and legally throughout history. It is not possible to "reduce" them to each other and to deal with the issue entirely. However, given the approaches of the political theory, which are quite intertwined today, the citizenship and the question of "…what is the being transmitted by this name and by its successive 'translations' " must first be given. It is seen to be clear that the association with "democracy", as one of the main facts of politics, in all the concept of citizenship. However, at this point, there is a serious matter according to Balibar, which is that there is a situation that should not be forgotten that "…there is an analogy arising from the contradiction between citizenship and democracy" (2016: 13–14). According to Yeatman, as a manifestation of this understanding, when an "ideal citizenship" is taken into consideration, it is the result of the human being as an individual resulting from an "integrated social life". In order for the citizen, who emerges as an integrated individual, to be integrated into the society, it is essential to offer a life in this sense. Here, it is clear that the individual stands out when dealing with the citizen. In this context, "individuality" is what requires its construction as a unique social action unit in all aspects of man. Taken through the individual, the "citizenship ideal" becomes something that can arise as a result of an integrated understanding of social humanity. Because, by uncovering a situation that enables the integration of the individual, it becomes easier for people to become citizens (2009: 103). In this way, the phenomenon of citizen, which has been handled through the individual, has been the subject of definitions through "individualism" from time to time. According to Sennett, who looks at the subject in this context, "individualism (in this case) is a peaceful and moderate feeling that leads each citizen to isolate himself from the people and the mass and to leave to the environment formed by his family and friends. Moreover, by constituting such a small society for his own comfort, one voluntarily withdraws from the affairs of the big society (2017: 136)".

Considering the above-mentioned citizenship within the framework of an individual-oriented ideal, it will be very difficult to conceptualize according to the ancient and modern period. For this reason, while trying to reposition citizenship within the framework of post-modern understanding, it is seen that its meaning can be revealed more clearly if it is subject to various evaluations by considering the historical and theoretical assumptions within the framework of the modern period.

When citizenship is considered within the framework of an ideal or evaluated in a modern sense, it is evolved into a socio-political legal form of identity in the process. Citizenship can only be the subject of evaluations as one of the forms of identity attributed to a person, which was discussed for about three hundred years. Citizenship is sometimes dominated by all identity approaches in this adventure while it is sometimes compressed into a historical meaning. Thus, citizenship faced a challenge to be used to describe the individual living in society in the history of the Western political thoughts and states. In the Western sources, while five "forms of identity" are brought to the fore in the context of regimes and social types, the historical process of citizenship is tried to be understood. These are "feudalism, monarchy, tyranny, nation, and citizenship", respectively. The situation at the end of these processes is that it depicts the basic network of relationships containing a "status" in which man is considered an "individual" as a social and political entity. In this sense, it is observed that the individual/s are shaped within the framework of a behavior pattern that determines those relationships and according to a system (Heater, 2007: 9).

Citizenship can also be described as the concept at the center of democratic practice, which is one of the "defining features of modernity" in the West. In this context, citizenship is a concept depending on modernity, "... people are equal in terms of dignity beyond their differences and material conditions, and that they have to be treated equally, both legally and politically..." At this point, the phenomenon of "equality" is brought to the fore and accepted as the "single" main actor of a political organization model that can succeed in keeping citizenship together (Schnapper, 1995: 10). The citizen that Schnapper handled in this way is moved to a dimension that should be handled as a "conscious" individual in the modern period. For this reason, the citizen is turned into a figure that is considered to be politically and socially important.

Individual, which is handled over four identities within the historical models of political organization other than modern citizenship with the classification of Heater, has always been discussed outside the concept of "equality". In these relations, a situation appears such as defining the individual by "hierarchical", "nationality", "supporting the regime with everything", and "sense of belonging", respectively. According to Heater, while the "belonging" of a group is always dominant in the position of the individual, the only identity definition of the individual firstly started with citizenship, which "tries to define the bond with the idea of the state", by the individual is removed out from a part of group. The individual in this citizenship idea has to be a "conscious being" automatically. Because, citizenship introduced as a new identity at this point has emerged as a new status, "hidden in the rights given by the state and all of them with equal status, as autonomous persons" and "hidden in the duties fulfilled by individuals" (Heater, 2007: 10). The determination of this status on behalf of citizenship has provided the basis of three different meanings expressed in terms of political, legal, and sociological perspectives in the modern period. This understanding is expressed as a *Marshallist*[10] perspective in citizenship debates. Especially when citizen is considered as a conscious

---

10 Thomas H. Marshall, an important professor of sociology at the London School of Economics, who lived between 1893 and 1982, is regarded as an important theoretician in the modern period with regard to this issue with his citizenship theory. In his work entitled *Citizenship and Social Development* (1963), Marshall wrote about the development process of citizenship in the modern period in the 18th century historically such as the acquisition of legal rights like fair trial, of political rights like voting right in the 19th century, and of welfare rights such as social security rights in the 20th century. Marshall, stating the courts of law, the parliament, and the welfare state as places where these rights developed, admitted that the developments at this point in the world marked a process parallel to the development of humanity along with the principles of welfare, class, and democracy. In this context, Marshall's thoughts about citizenship have been criticized from time to time by being an evolutionist with Anglo-centrism and by ignoring the understanding of industrial democracy in the development of citizenship rights. However, Marshall, by influencing important sociologists such as Robert Merton, S. M. Lipset, and Ralf Dahrendorf, has still an important place in citizenship discussions today (Marshall, 1999: 475).

entity, it has reached a stage where these three expressions "unite" by Marshall combined. Citizenship, determined as a result of these three, has overcome the important problem in evaluating society as "included" or "excluded". Citizenship, which is widely defined in this process, is also the subject of evaluations in the context of "human rights". Citizenship has thus been embraced with a meaning that includes political, legal, and sociological perspectives having "all kinds of rights and obligations regarding membership in social groups and organizations" (Mindus, 2009: 33–34).

This concept, theoretically introduced by Marshall in the 19th century, is closely related to the economic, political, and social adventure experienced by the Western individual in the last four centuries. It is said that the "modern" change and transformation in especially economy, which human beings experience, have been determinant at this point when compared to the pre-industrial period. In this sense; within the beginning of the modern period, there is a peasant society living, producing, and consuming by themselves in its own villages by a social structure that can be considered autonomous. On the other hand, however, it is also a case that a "capitalism" has begun, which grows with a market economy that constantly produces and spreads in contradiction to this extent and initiates the formation of the society in which we live. This situation gave birth to a dual life style experienced at the same time but being foreign to each other, yet which can be explained by their relationships and compulsory unity, and it has carried this process to the present day (Braudel, 2017: 12–13). Some authors seek to the beginning of this process in the events experienced during the 17th century. The most important example in this process is "the British Civil War", which is seen as a result of social fights in England. The British Civil War is an important turning point in the social "mixed change process" in the West. Especially the social, political, and economic events taking place in England during the civil war and accepted to go parallel to the war are important. What happened in this process represented an irreversible transformation in the Western world, as a "modern and secular society, in a feudal and religious order having grown strong and knurled all the way, going slowly by opening its path". This period was seen as "a very clear indication that trade gained increasing importance in both rural areas" and cities starting from the fourteenth century and that feudalism was replaced by England's rather weak absolute monarchy and

accepted that the events in the 19th century are the most important stage
of transition to the modern period (Moore, 2003: 30–31).

It is seen that citizenship started to be discussed in modern times as a
result of the political, social, and economic developments explained over
Britain as the most obvious example, while going to a new world. It is
certain that the administrative regimes in monarchic, aristocratic, and oli-
garchic terms for centuries are parallel to the beginning of criticism during
the 17th and 18th centuries. It is seen that there was a wear on traditional
views within the framework of nobility, wealth, and "right to manage"
of the powerful. Because the understandings that the ruling authority is
based on the God, heredity, or power has begun to experience a crisis of
"legitimacy". The coming of democratic understanding to the fore point,
which is the manifestation of an ancient thought with citizenship, coincided
with the same times in this time of period. In this time, opinions such as no
one can declare themselves "sovereign" or "cannot claim an unconditional
power claim" started to find supporters again. In the West, "the understanding that the source of the authority to manage can only be legitimized
by relying on the ruled (the people) has started to settle" gradually. It is
seen that many thinkers contribute to the shaping and development of this
view within the framework of different perspectives (Uygun, 2017: 175).
In this case, the discussion of the individual figure through citizenship as
one of the main actors of the political systems found a suitable ground in
the West as a plane.

Along with the criticism of traditionally accepted views, shaping the
citizen in the West in the context of status discussions in the society has
also led to an important problem area. The value attributed to citizenship,
especially as an important asset in modern society, has made it a very controversial phenomenon. The primary issue at this point that came to the
fore was "education". In the process of the educational development of
modern central states and the strengthening of the legal systems of these
structures established on a national basis, the "primary school" institution
played a "transformative" role. This institution has been one of the most
important recipes of "building" processing of the "ruling elites" since the
second half of the 18th century. With the second half of the same century,
the process of "secularization" and "laicization" in the Western world,
both individually and socially, accelerated. Because, for the new political

structures, "the human and citizen model" needed by the ruling elite as a result of the laicization of the use of the source of sovereignty and the secularization of the state in some places within the framework of "national sovereignty" against the understanding of sovereignty originated from the God has been an important cornerstone (Üstel, 2005: 11). Especially in the whole 19th century and the first quarter of the 20th century, the "national sovereignty principle" developed, with national independence movements that seemed to develop primarily in Europe and then spread all over the world. This principle has been handled within the framework of democracy demands and has been evaluated in terms of citizenship. In fact, when it came to the First World War, the phenomenon of nation started to be seen "as a tool to preserve the truly human side of man, that is the autonomy represented by values of equality and freedom". While forming the nation phenomenon, it is seen that the citizen is based on it. In the basic evaluation of the nation, it was based on the participation of all citizens in state activities. Moreover, it is a claim that the demands of minorities like language, etc. are the result of requests to join the state and contribute to it. In this way, the handling of citizenship in a socially integrated manner has been strongly studied. It is tried to think of the notion of "modern nation", which is dealt with in various ways, on the "equality" ideal, based on citizenship (Schnapper, 1995: 17).

It is observed that the citizenship literature has evolved considerably and theoretically throughout the 21st century. It is seen that citizenship, which should be considered on nation and modern values, is tried to be handled in four different ways in the literature:

"1. Citizenship defined as national identity or nationality,
2. Citizenship defined on the basis of documents,
3. Citizenship defined on the basis of rights,
4. Citizenship defined on the basis of duties and responsibilities (Kadıoğlu, 2008c: 21)".

Modern citizen, which is the subject of a formal assessment as a state-related entity in these four ways, has now been the subject of discussion on different topics in dimension of the citizen. It is also a case that discussions about the re-evaluation of the citizen "as a conscious being", even though it is subject to certain classifications, are discussed strongly in the West. Especially in the literature, it can be seen that the discussions about the "freedoms" of the individual and the societies have been opened in the historical sense in order to become a conscious citizen. The concept of "freedom" has been brought to the fore in order for citizenship to express something other than the Western individual in the classification of Heater that the history before him was expressed in four ways. Since the history of Rome, individuals have been evaluated as free individuals and slaves. The free individual here is used to meet the person who has a "status" against the state and on a social basis. This free individual has been described as "a *civis*, a citizen with all its implications for the protection from interference" (Pettit, 1998: 55). Starting from the point showed by Pettit, it is possible to talk about citizens as a conscious being accepted in the Western intellectual and academic literature in terms of the community of political individuals, especially in some meanings stated by Gianfranco Poggi:

> "... points to a very important element of citizenship politically: *Citizens as political participants/partisans*. (This situation) means "to join", "to take sides", "to be partisanized", and "to seek the way to defend the interests of others"...With the political maneuver of the political rhetoric...in today's conditions, *citizens as viewers*, (in this sense) citizens refuse or try to reduce as much as possible the problem of partisanship –including the price of learning about complex issues, they think that a certain degree of political occupation can only be excused where alternatives they can use in their spare time can compete –especially with their interest in the media–...(Finally) *citizens as equals*. This highlights the crucial significance of the symbolically charged contribution of the revolutionary France on behalf of the *citoyen*: Individuals see and wish to be seen as persons having equal value with others and sharing certain basic rights. One of them –perhaps Marshall neglected– is the right to a certain degree of respect and right to acceptance that cannot be ignored. With a Durkheimian or Goffman approach, all citizens are to some extent sacred objects, only as citizens (2011: 46–47)".

It is understood from Poggi's approach that the first characteristic of the individual, who is qualified as a conscious citizen, is an individual who has guarantees at certain points and above all should not be in a "slave" structure. In this context, there have been some developments, especially in the Western world throughout the 19th century. In this process, it is known that citizenship developed in three different frameworks in order to become a conscious entity. These are, in line with Marshall's views, is the development process of citizenship within the framework of civil, political, and social rights. Citizenship developing in the axis of civil rights includes the rights and freedoms such as "individual freedom, freedom of speech, freedom of thought and belief, right to possession, right to contract, and right to justice". In this context, it is also important to "secure it in the basis of right to justice, individual rights, equality and law". For this reason, it is stated that the institutions concerning civil rights are "civil courts". Within the framework of political rights, rights mean to participate "as the voters and elected in the political decision making process". In this context, finally, social rights include a wide scale of rights ranging from "having rights such as economic welfare and social security to the right to be able to live like a modern individual". In this dimension, "education right and social services" are also assessed within the framework of social rights (Marshall and Bottomore, 2000: 21). It is a case in which individuals raised in the nation-state understanding develop a level of awareness based on these rights. Even though it contains some changes, transformations, and differentiations for this reason, the awareness levels of modern citizen today should be evaluated based on loyalty to the rights listed above.

The "rights" towards citizenship, which comes to the forefront in terms of gaining a conscious structure of an individual, bring forward the developments considered in the "social rights" dimension in the political and ideological context. These rights are broadened in general within the framework of "civil, political and social rights" that form the basis of modern citizenship. At the end of the process, it is observed that the discussions on the social rights dimension of modern citizenship becomes more meaningful depending on "welfare state policies" and "democratic participation" (Kadıoğlu, 2008c: 26).

Especially in the English-speaking countries, those of much of what was experienced in the 19th and 20th centuries have been focused on democratic representation governments. The developments related to this issue have led to the emergence of many institutions and understandings which societies need and could be accepted as new in the name of human history. Although this situation shows various differences in its constitutional structures in the Western plane, it is tried to be discussed through the similarities of the basic political institutions that show a parallel development. These are according to Dahl:

- "Important government decisions and policies are implemented directly or indirectly by the authorities determined through general elections or responsibility in this context is assumed by these persons.
- Citizens are entitled to participate freely with fair elections that are reasonably repeated; but they are not obliged to attend.
- Citizens can be candidates for elected tasks and they can serve by undertaking these tasks; however, age and place of residence imperatives may be attached to these tasks.
- Citizens can express their views on a wide range of political issues in the public arena, without the threat of serious punishment.
- All citizens have the right to access independent news through other citizens, newspapers and many other sources; moreover, there are news sources that are not under the control of the government or a particular group, and their content is under the effective protection of the law.
- Contrary to the prevailing view that political factions are a danger to be avoided in earlier democracies and republics; both in theory and in practice, it has been emphasized that they have to have the right to establish relatively independent associations and organizations that contain independent parties and interest groups in order to fulfill the requirements of various rights of citizens (2018: 23)".

When citizenship is addressed through the framework outlined above, it is a general acceptance that the important problem areas related to political and social issues and the solution suggestions related to them are concentrated after a certain stage of the century. However, there is a clear situation that efforts towards this issue are directed towards the problem areas discussed within the framework of the Western norms and many of them are solved within the framework of the Western norms. Because the historical process of the phenomenon of "citizenship" formed in the Western norms and the understanding of *"social nation state (l'Etat national-social)"* could not be able to solve inequalities in the world, including what is considered as the "North" and "South" problems. The Western solution processes, which were considered together with the "neo-liberal" policies implemented in the last quarter of the 20th century, especially in the dimension of "social rights", turned out to be too shallow not to be applied in certain geographies around the world. It is seen that this was the biggest problem in the name of the "universal formation" of a conscious citizen understanding. In this sense, the main problem in the absence of an understanding of citizenship for the whole world is the paradoxes that "criticism of formal constitutionalism has brought up the issue of *controversial democracy* that should be discussed universally, that is comparatively (Balibar, 2016: 59)".

When establishing a conscious citizen was started to be handled in the discussions of "democracy", it appears that human beings had not the only problem area during the modern period in terms of the Western world and the world in general. If the issue can be viewed from a different window, it can be better understood why it is discussed differently between the West and the other world in the name of citizenship and awareness of citizenship. Therefore, it is seen that the controversial areas related to citizenship can be explained by some specific developments in the modern period. In the period after the American and French Revolutions, citizenship is seen as a poem of "rights". Along with the modern republic administrations established by the destruction of many important absolute monarchy state structures in the world, especially France, the way for citizens to move freely in a conscious way was opened. In other words, with the developments in France after the French Revolution, it was possible to put citizenship rights in a frame. With the constitutional guarantee of the concept of equality, it was seen that citizens were defined as a conscious structure based on "unity of interests" within a "public" entirety. The design of citizenship has reached a point by reassessing its position in the state within the framework of an understanding of "sovereignty" in the modern age (Audier, 2006: 47–56).

In the last 250–300 years' period of humanity, we face a situation where solutions to many political and social events in the world can be addressed in connection with the conjunctional situation of the period or the countries. Therefore, it is understandable why citizenship is not a problem area at the same time for the whole world. When the issue is examined at this point, it is seen that the citizenship experiences cannot be handled at the same level of development and progress even for the whole West. However, focusing on the issue of citizenship as a conscious being, at least theoretically, some important data can be obtained in the thought of the French Revolution and the Anglo-Saxon only a century ago. As discussed in detail in the first part of the study, it is seen that the "citizen as a status" approach, which is believed to have developed after the mid-17th century, is a political fact. Although this is not thought to solve many problems in the context of status, it is an important milestone in civic debates, and the subject is still being discussed over many concepts which were put forward at that time (Oldfield, 2008: 97).

Even though the determination of the prominent thoughts on this point were limited in the name of the political regimes of that day, their impact on contemporary debates was theoretically and practically strong. Even today, the views of G. W. F. Hegel (1770–1831), who wrote the most important sources of that period on the state and citizens, are still discussed. The views of Hegel, who is one of the strong representatives of the idea that the whole meaning of humanity originates from the state, has not been definitively refuted today. The divinized state and patriotism-based nationalism were united by Hegel, and the idea that a citizen who could not find a legal place in this structure could not exist as a human was opened to discussion. According to Hegel, an individual can gain an identity only when being a member of a nation-state. At a time when this understanding was dominant, it was seen that the concept of modern citizenship emerged through the nation-state. In this period, the citizen started to be used for people who have a national identity consciousness and have responsibilities towards their nation, and also who "are aware" of these responsibilities. In this use, the citizen is generally taken in a way that indicates a more valuable and conscious phenomenon than the individuals who constitute the public. In this sense, it is observed that the citizen can form some legal and political legitimacy (Kadıoğlu, 2008c: 22). It can be seen that the process experienced theoretically and practically by nation-states in 19th century with Hegel is important in revealing the citizen in a modern sense. It is certain that the developing ideological understandings at this point nourish the thought. Citizenship has gained importance "in the evaluation of the individual as a social entity", especially when socialism has come to the fore in the discussions of equality and social freedom. In this context, "drawing attention to the ideas of cooperation, reciprocity, and fraternity that more appropriately express the social ties that should be between people" has brought discussions to a new dimension for a conscious citizenship (Oldfield, 2008: 97).

It is not a coincidence that it is 19th century when is the century of nation and ideologies as the era on which the development of citizenship started to be defined on this meaning and use is based. By the 19th century, the rights of citizens have developed in a way that includes both individual freedom and solidarity feelings with the influence of liberal values and partly socialist thoughts on the world, especially the Western states. Citizenship has strengthened in the point of awareness based on "constitutional rights and responsibilities" along with "protective and egalitarian" themes. Especially the work *Democracy in America* by Alexis de Tocqueville (1805–1859) showed how citizenship can be evaluated with an egalitarian understanding in democratic and republican modern societies. The theoretical and practical analysis of Tocqueville on the political and legal framework of the United States is important. Tocqueville examined the importance of civic participation in the social structure and the importance of a free community of citizens for the stability of the system. Tocqueville's views on a significant emphasis for peace of society are valuable for addressing citizenship as a conscious being. Tocqueville's characterization of social organization and struggles for rights as a right under constitutional guarantee without contradiction with traditions and customs is an important determination for the development process of the modern civilization approach in the Western thought (Audier, 2006: 57–59).

The phenomenon of "rights" towards the citizen, which developed throughout the 19th century, turned into the "citizen rights" that we use today as a result of a discourse. In this context, if the civil rights have evolved "in the context of expressing the demands of individuals as natural beings as possible, not civilized", it leads to the discussion of the issue in a historical dimension that "the emergence of the question of who owns these rights". The main reason for this discussion is that, as previously mentioned, the term of 'citizenship' is a notion of the period in which the Roman city culture existed. However, although the term " 'ius' or 'right' to be applied to individuals" in the Roman Law was used throughout history, it is certain that this definition does not fully meet the concept of "rights" in the modern period. Because, it is seen that both morality and legal philosophy of Rome basically "have a function preventing the demand of natural man in a civil context in different ways". At this point, Cicero's views were brought to the fore. Cicero, in his work called *De Inventione*, especially emphasized that humanity is living a "wild" life in its natural form. Cicero argued that people should be "civilized through reason and rhetoric". While Cicero was in this idea, the emphasis that the citizen was superior to natural man as a moral being in Rome has been used in modern times for a long time (Brett, 2011: 116). However, at this point, it emerges that there is a fundamental understanding difference between the notion of "rights" of the modern human citizen understanding and the rights of the Roman citizen. Because, in the citizenship approach discussed within the framework of the liberal view, the present freedoms have been developed in a way that basically includes the idea of "rights", and freedom and "human rights" have begun to be treated as a result of respect for the individual. In this new understanding, it is accepted that rights sometimes contribute to "political freedom" and sometimes to "economic freedom". According to liberal thought; these sometimes complement each other, sometimes they occur in a way intertwined in many respects (Melnik, 2006: 11). For this reason, the effects of economic and social changes cannot be ignored in the discussions on the modern citizen to be a conscious entity. Thus, it is seen that evaluating the event only from historical facts causes some problems in terms of assessing the subject in a modern sense.

The discussions about the citizenship on historical and sometimes occa-sional practices focus on revealing the basic facts of the freedom of the citizen as a conscious being throughout the 19th century. However, many issues can be understood when the process of paradoxical development in the political and economic dimension in the transition to the modern period is treated in comparison with England and France. Colin Mooers' findings regarding the formation and development process of the bourgeois are important for the political and social debates in the West:

> "... If what in England is a "classical" bourgeois revolution, France represents an occasional situation. As in the UK, the coalition of the bourgeoisie for the small producers was a vital factor in the overthrow of the *ancien régime*. But in France, in terms of capitalism, both the small producers and the bourgeoisie developed much less. However, the political character of the revolution was in a sense much more developed. Compared to the British Revolution, urban and peasant masses were mobilized more intensively and continuously. This was partly due to the fact that the old class, partly dominant, stood firmly in more places than in England. The fact that the large bourgeois sections cling to the same extent within the structures of the absolute state, to a lesser extent, was complicating the situation more. Of course, this is closely related to the form it took in the early stages of the revolution; because the bourgeois was increas-ingly facing the threat of exclusion from political authorities, "politics" was in great demand.

Again, the fact that the revolution was 'politically developed early' was a precursor to a pattern that would become much more ordinary in the nineteenth century. As the undeveloped societies tried to bridge the gap with more developed capitalist countries, the state became the natural ideological center of those who wanted to improve their competitiveness in a relatively short period of time (2000: 214)".

The understanding of modern social development above can become meaningful, especially by examining the political and economic developments in France in the formation process of modern citizenship. The subject was evaluated through the processes related to "the nature of the individual" and "the quality of social ties" between citizens as "individuals", under the influence of the liberal view in France. In this context, it was enabled to discuss a new understanding of "social citizenship" in modern sense. In France, a theoretical infrastructure was prepared for citizenship through the conceptualizations of "liberal" or "liberal-individualist" and "classic" or "citizen-based republican"[11]. At this point, it is not claimed that the two

---

11 Human was seen as "citizens of the whole world or the city of God" in the Greek city states classically, firstly, and then in the Hellenistic period and Rome, and thereafter in the Christian world. At this point, the reconsideration of the citizen has been moved to the modern era with this classical understanding coming back to the agenda in the Renaissance Europe. The citizen was considered to be of the Roman origin rather than the Aristotelian Greek perspective. The citizen that Machiavelli deals with is of the Roman origin with its heroes and development. In the works of Machiavelli on the Roman Republic, the reason for the greatness of Rome was the virtue Roman citizens. According to Machiavelli, it is essential to reconsider the "freedom" concept, which is the basis of law and politics in Rome, which is the reason for the strength and stability of Rome, in order to prevent the fragility of Florence, of which he is a citizen. This understanding of freedom had two dimensions; "Resistance from attacks by other states and the absence of tyranny of any person or class" and the virtue of citizenship. Citizen virtue, for him, is "self-discipline, patriotism, submission, and willingness to give up personal gains for the sake of public benefit". The thoughts taking place within "the classical republicanism" together with Machiavelli and handled within the framework of "liberal-individualist" and "citizen-based republicanism", were the issues addressed in the vast majority of many political and social debates that lasted from 16th century until the 19th century. However, this understanding has been criticized most of the time because it has a "retrospective" point of view "taking the Roman Republic as a political ideal". But, the Roman

concepts are completely separated from each other. However, when evaluated through these two models, it is understood that the need to rely on different theoretical foundations to solve the legal and political problems of citizenship on a social basis emerges (Oldfield, 2008: 93). Citizenship, evaluated entirely over a "status" in "liberal individualism", is mentioned on the individual having brought to a weak position by governments as the executive of the states. In "citizen-based republicanism", citizenship is considered as a "practice". It is thought that the opportunities that citizenship can obtain as a practical approach can be weakened by the governments in this way, which are the executive body of the states, and so citizenship in republicanism is emphasized as a "public" entity. At this point, contrary to the liberal understanding, it is seen that citizen-based republicanism makes a serious effort to solve the problems of the modern individual. However, both liberal individualism and citizen-based republicanism are essentially contributing to the modern citizenship's survival as a conscious being, whether they bring to the fore either the aspects of status or the "social solidarity" (Oldfield, 2008: 94–95). Because these schools, which are still

---

thought, in the republican conceptions of many important thinkers, from Bernard Mandeville (1670–1733) to J. J. Rousseau, was seen as a contribution to "simplicity of life", "compulsive public spirits", and "self-management". Some thinkers are discussed the suitability of the ancient Roman citizen to the French people in the 18th century world. Some authors, especially Benjamin Constant (1767–1830), thought that it was necessary to draw a "moral" lesson after the French Revolution's failure to reproduce the republican virtue in practice. According to them, "ancient citizenship and freedom were political and participatory". It required self-discipline and simplicity. This was only possible in warrior, small states. However, contemporary freedom was the freedom of the individual, not the citizen. It meant freedom in politics and against politics. The contemporary man had lost something, but earned a lot. For example, "prosperity, individuality, and peace". This situation is important in the acceptance of important arguments for the discussion of the citizen as an entity in terms of "voting right", "employment", and "economy" after the 19th century especially. In this process, parallel to Benjamin Constant's views, the idea of "positive freedom" was discussed within the republican tradition, and it was developed a thought that sees "freedom of democratic participation" above all in the name of citizenship (Miller et al., 1995: 457–459; Pettit, 1998: 40, 49, 267).

at the forefront of today's discussions, are the main sources of reference for addressing the dimension of "individual rights" of citizenship.

Many citizenship conceptions, which were shaped theoretically as above, were diversified as a result of ideological diversity in the end of 19th century and the 20th century. Efforts to form a conscious citizen, aware of their constitutional guarantees in many Western states, evolved into a citizenship model compatible with the developing and transforming human profile. In this context, the most important commitment of all political structures accepting themselves as a liberal democracy is them to be going to be equal and free citizens. No matter to which group, class or community they belong, they are promised to their citizens by Western governments and other world states to be provided basic civil and political rights for individuals. This became a discourse reflected in all kinds of constitutional rights declarations (Kymlicka, 1998: 71).

The concept of "nation", which we emphasized before, underwent a development process in parallel with these processes. Because when looking at the development of the concept of nation, this was matched with the concept of citizenship and started to treat with it. But the nation, in the 20th century, took on a dynamic character with the ideological and political arguments, but not consistently. For example, for Hannah Arendt (1906–1975), it is a paradoxical result of the nation's occupation by the state. In the modern period, the reason is why the law instrument was identified with an indefinite way from the state and the nation instrument was together with the state. Thus, it was emphasized that the essential nations of the state were more easily accepted and recognized by the state. Because, by the 20th century, the link between the state and the nation evolved into a more intertwined process than ever before (Isin & Turner, 2009: 11–12). Particularly, most democratic and republican regimes marking the formation phase of the century modern states system are nation-state structures of the 20th century, and citizenship in this process emerged as a "unique way of organizing and living political and social membership... moving from an institutional and social psychological reality". Individuals also tried to establish their citizenship through the bond they established with nations. Another reality is that nation-states structurally and mentally challenged a situation such as "egalitarian, sacred, national, democratic, single, and socially important" (Brubaker,

2008: 56). Some authors addressed this situation in terms of "being an involuntary entity belonging to a nation" and explained the citizenship in the process of becoming a nation with the criteria developed without considering the "volunteerism" approach of "membership" understanding. According to this understanding, the individual here does not choose to be "belonging", but by can become a citizen, gaining "belonging" (Margalit & Raz, 1990: 447). This perspective transforms the handling of a nation-state citizen into a very clear and precise process over belonging to nation. However, it is seen that this understanding is a thought that treats with the nation-state and the citizen together and is concerned only with one aspect of the subject. Because, based on many political and social areas of debate today, it is ambiguous whether the process of forming a bond of citizenship can be explained so clearly or not.

Nation-states, as discussed above, contain many systematically compelling elements, as many thinkers emphasize. However, nation-states are still the only political structures that can act steadily in the complex world of today in providing and maintaining health, social, security, and educational rights for their citizens, especially when Western countries are addressed. In addition, the nation-state understanding continues to be the only structural institution that could take concrete steps to provide "welfare" rights in line with the conditions of the country for the formation of a citizen as a modern conscious individual.

The rights developed for the purpose of the welfare of the citizen have been evaluated within the context of the development of "social" awareness. In this sense, it can be said that this phenomenon is decisive in conscious citizenship discussions. At this point, social rights, which have a certain difference from the civil and political rights as we have discussed before, are handled together with the "quality of life" phenomenon, which describes the nature of today's modern man. It is discussed today as the most important citizen rights that access to healthcare services and education opportunities, which are believed to be achieved by the individual on a community basis. In addition, it is accepted that the freedom and equality that will arise with the acquisition of civil and political rights today cannot be achieved without reaching social rights. It is Thomas Humprey Marshall, who paved the way for discussion of the issue by evaluating the citizenship rights of today with a broad understanding.

Marshall's thoughts on this issue were considered as important opinions especially for the development of social rights and the citizen's becoming a conscious being at this point (Heater, 2007: 171–172). The reason for this characterization is that the welfare forms of Marshall's thought of citizenship are based on social rights. As a result of this situation, individuals contribute to the state in certain ways, such as military service or similar public responsibilities. Tax and retirement are also two important economic institutions related to citizenship defined by Marshall. According to him, tax evasion and bribery are signs of state lowness. It is important that the state is strong in this dimension. Economist John Maynard Keynes (1883–1946) came to the fore in solving problems such as tax evasion and bribery. Keynes' welfare economy and Marshall's understanding of citizenship caused some changes in the labor market in the West and around the world. These thoughts transformed modern welfare, pulled down the traditional family, reduced pension funds, weakened the understanding of gender-based division of labor among workers, and changed the reproduction of productive technologies (Isin & Turner, 2009: 9).

Especially the transformation experienced with the developments in the last 50 years, the determination of citizenship status, and anomalies for citizenship access for non-citizens and their descendants in a country have become a rule-based routine. In this context, the sharp character of the modern and state-based citizenship concept has been transformed in certain meanings and has lost its character of nationalism. It is important that the logic of individual rights can be maintained within the framework of citizenship status and entered into a more systematic area at the discretion of a state under the influence of international law. Ethnic, racial, and cultural restrictions have been largely abolished within the framework of today's state understandings. It can be stated that citizenship is no longer exempt from sociological prevalence, but is also at the stage of assessment at the point of its multiple identities, which is also challenged by people's differentiation process (Joppke, 2009: 38–39). It is certain that these developments, which express a new situation, form important parameters regarding the sustainability of citizenship as a conscious entity or whether or not the citizens level of social rights for changes, negatively or positively.

Citizenship, which stays at the conditions of the formation of a democratic notion in theoretical and practical terms as a result of the developments, has found itself in the current discussions in many crises of the modern age. But the modern world has undergone political, social, and cultural changes and transformations with the triggering of the economic crises experienced in the last quarter of the 20th century. The content of the concept has been somewhat influenced, especially as regards citizenship as a conscious entity. In this context, the findings of E. Fuat Keyman are remarkable:

"These breakdowns, which become more evident and visible with the effects of postmodernization and globalization processes, mean the weakening of assumed links between citizenship and nation-state, citizenship and ethnos, and citizenship and demos in modern societies. Citizenship enters into a serious process of change with the opening of ethnos and demos to others coming from inside and outside and criticizing the dominant understanding of us. As others make demands on new rights and freedoms, it also raises the need to expand the interior place of the modern citizenship concept built on us. The concept of citizenship is re-established in the context of its content and meaning, and this re-establishment process reveals the re-establishment of democracy through a pluralistic and multicultural understanding of demos. While this simultaneous re-establishment relationship between citizenship and democracy is increasing the interest in the concept of citizenship in academic and public discourse on the other hand, it strengthens the idea that the solution to identity-based conflicts can be in the field of citizenship through democratic negotiation on the other hand (2008: 7)".

As it can be understood from the passage above; democratic structures have differentiated in terms of "establishing reliable legal principles" in general, unlike many traditional regimes operating over "mass asymmetry, oppression, exploitation, and patronage" for centuries within the framework of the developments, in the last quarter of the 20th century. According to Charles Tilly, the universal acceptance of the Western liberal values came to the agenda, especially due to the collapse of the Socialist Bloc in the world in 1989. In this context, Tilly stated that a system can be accepted as a democracy, if it provides the following criteria for its citizens:

"1. The entity of regular and precise relations, not intermittent and individual, between the state and citizens (e.g., legal residence alone establishes routine relationships with government institutions, whether they are with certain bosses or members in certain ethnic groups; it doesn't matter);

2. These relationships include all or most of the citizens (e.g., there are no considerable independently surrounded areas within the borders of the state);

3. These relationships are equal in the general of citizens and citizen categories (e.g., based on gender, religion, and wealth; no one's right to vote or duty can be legally removed);

4. State staff, resources, and activities vary depending on the binding joint consultation of citizens (e.g., a law is made by a public referendum);

5. Citizens, especially minority members, are protected from the arbitrary practices of state officials (e.g., every individual, regardless of social category, may seek his/her right before imprisonment) (Tilly, 2008: 199–200)".

III Today's Citizen as an "Aware" Entity Defined Through "Interests" and "Common Equalities"

The nation-state, which is the determining element of citizenship during the modern period, enters into a process that experiences discusses "a new world order, difference, demand for certain rights, and a fragmented civil society" in the post-modern period from the areas where "equality, universal rights, and a solid civil society" are theoretically determined. Post-modern or global era discussions treated within the framework of the concept of "justice" on a universal basis focuses on "the tension between political equality and cultural difference" arising from global interaction and interdependence. It is certain that globalization offers a new perspective to concepts such as "citizenship, rights, and publicity" in the modern period (Vega, 2011: 135). One of the most important discussion areas of the facts of citizens and citizenship of this period is the question "what is important for the citizen?" and the search for a clear answer to this question. This shows that the citizen, as a conscious being, needs new definitions. In this process, the questions "how is citizenship?" or "how do people gain citizenship?" are raised. In the answer of these questions, it is seen that a citizen is turned into an "individual" who can be isolated from a social being "from actions towards actions" and who are able to act on his own. In this way, the citizen as a conscious entity evolves from a phenomenon seen in certain actions to a "process that can encompass a number of different activities" (Asen, 2004: 191).

Although it seems to be discussed in a more complicated and individual dimension compared to the modern period, it is seen that the citizenship debate is opened to discussion again and with quite different definitions. One of the most important reasons for this is seen as the changing nature of citizenship. One of the main elements in the political structure of the modern state in relation to capitalism is considered citizenship. The solution of the "state-citizen" equation is an important problem area especially in the new social structure thought together with post-industrial society capitalism. Citizenship in new discussions is seen as the concept of a different dimension. The citizen considered as a new product of the post-modern era is both a phenomenon and an entity while it is a term that tends to be transformed terminologically. So much so that citizenship starts to be presented to humanity as a multi-dimensional and contentious concept. In this context, the citizen is a "differentiated", "multicultural", "hybrid", and "supranational" being, and it is identified with the "world". In other words, the citizen is seen far above all the political, social, legal, and economic data of the modern era that are considered as holistic with the nation, and it is desired to be transformed into an asset excluded from the data (White, 2009: 7).

The opening of the nation-state understanding to the debate in recent years has shaken modern political structures that are thought to have fallen into a serious crisis of "legitimacy". In this process, many political facts in which include citizenship have started to be discussed through the fields mentioned above. While it makes all modern values and institutions open to questioning, including the understanding of "the reconstruction of capitalism for societies", which is thought to have started in Europe at the end of World War II especially, "citizenship identity" has also been questioned in all its dimensions (Gündüz and Gündüz, 2007: 5). Dominique Schnapper, who reads this subject in contrary to the spirit of the period and completely over the problem of "being a nation", explained the source of the problem today as follows:

> "... (Today) approximately half of the national law falls into a jurisdiction shared between the national state and the community.
>
> But in addition to these interdependencies of modern societies, identities, political and symbolic identifications and individuals' "moral life" (Mauss) differ greatly from one nation to another. Today, the objective integration of people in a virtually universal area leads to a contradiction with their social habitus, feelings of collective identity, and political participation continuing to be very high at the national level (1995: 198)".

When considered in this context, the current position of the citizen, which is the subject of certain evaluations, is that it is an element in terms of political socialization. Citizens are considered here within the framework of "awareness of forming a political community". The phenomenon of consciousness is that the citizen has a certain knowledge in political social-ization about political symbols, institutions, and procedures. In this way, the citizen learns the process of becoming a passive or active member of the administration. In this way, the citizen internalizes the social structure through certain value systems or completes "the process of placing into the political system" using certain ideological devices. At this point, political socialization can be perceived both as an individual learning process and as a cultural spread of the community as a consciousness (Marshall, 1999: 666). Because human, as an individual, undergoes a "socialization process" in the society where s/he lives with social institutions such as people, family, school, and work environment. At the end of this process, what is called 'citizenship' becomes a role learned and taught. Therefore, it can be thought that citizenship is a result of social relations and interaction in the context of both conscious and social roles. Understanding how awareness is formed in an effort to understand citizenship depends on understanding how citizenship roles are perceived and experienced by individuals. At this point, it is important to investigate the social and political projections of citizenship by considering them on an individual basis. Because this issue can be seen as an important argument in measuring the levels of "consciousness" among citizens (Caymaz, 2007: 4). This state of awareness becomes more meaningful when considered from a different perspective that should not be ignored. From Ronald Dworkin's point of view, citizenship is like a comprehensive and collective orchestra of human acts within the framework of modern social integration approaches within today's jargon. According to Dworkin, this is as follows in detail:

"Integration says that the real actor is not an individual, but a community to which he belongs, in some actions affecting the individual's peace. The individual is ethically connected to this actor: As an individual, s/he shares the successes or failures of acts, actions or practices that can be independent of everything he does. E.g., most Germans born after the WWII carry the embarrassment of the Nazis' monstrosity and feel the imperative to compensate them... (According to this case) a good orchestra itself is an actor. The musicians who compose it are proud of an individual victory; they are proud of the performance of the orchestra as a whole, not because of their individual brilliant musical abilities or capacities. It is this orchestra that succeeds or fails. And the success or failure of this orchestra is the success or failure of each of its members.

So integration is quite different from altruism and paternalism. It is also different from the pride or regret felt as either representative or indirect. When the parent is proud of the success of their children or when the friends are mutually proud of their own success... the actor, who is the actor of the acts that causes

pride or joy or dishonesty, is the individual himself. The enthusiasm that we feel
for the other is a secondary, parasitic enthusiasm. Success and failure, accom-
plishment or misfortune differ from each other. And the benefit we take here
does not show that we participate in an action; it reflects our special relationship with the actor.

The argument for integration is out of my objections to the argument against
paternalism; because in the whole of the argument for integration, apart from
my objections to the paternalist argument; because in the whole of the argument for integration, it rejects structure of action and benefit on which the
paternalist argument is built. The argument for integration prohibits us to think
in Mill's term, that is, the question of whether we intervene to protect other
people or the agent itself from the damage caused by the agent's behaviors. It
rejects such an individualized form of thought as a whole. In the opinion of the
argument for integration, the actor is the community itself. And it only asks
how the community's decisions on freedom and regulation will affect the life of
the *community* and its character. It emphasizes that the life of citizens coincides
with the life of the community, and it is not possible to grasp the special form of
self–directed success and failures of individual lives. Then, the hidden person-
ification in the idea of integration is original and deep. It is based on ordinary
ideas, actors, and ideas of individual utility about altruism, paternalism, and
enthusiasm that empathy leads. Integration offers a very different conceptual
structure. The basic element in this structure is not the individual, but the community itself.

According to all of these, integration causes a baroque metaphysics which
argues that communities are the basic entity in the universe and that individual
human beings are nothing but abstractions and illusions. But integration can
be comprehended differently, not depending on the ontological feature of the
community, but as daily and ordinary events in the social practices of human
beings (2006: 278–279)".

According to the views of Dworkin, it is seen that citizenship awareness is
formed as a result of the processes experienced by human beings as a social
individual, whether radical or rational. Today, every industrialized society
becomes a pluralist in many industrial, economic, and cultural contexts.
This situation paves the way for the emergence of societies that can be established through "interest groups", although the awareness of community
building is primarily addressed on an individual basis. The modern citizen
is the most important and decisive being in society, but it is sought such
answers whether or not individuals with healthy community awareness
in democracy can be raised in new pluralist societies. Because in the new
social structures, it is accepted that there is a "conflicting interests balance"

that makes it difficult for a certain group to dominate the system. This situation is deemed important both in affecting the government's activities and it is thought that it paves the way for a society consisting of competitive communities with economic activities (Roskin et al., 2013: 206–207). The formation of this idea is important in that it shows that the formation of a consciousness among citizens is a matter of debate in today's world.

Citizen comes to the forefront in today's discussions to be a more conscious entity. But citizenship is seen as a result of a mixed network of political, social, economic, and even technological dimensions in the modern period. In this context, the citizen is defined as a "free" entity that can have general and special will and moves away from being a concept that expresses a certain legal status in the classical periods. Thus, the citizen becomes a concept that can also be used to mean and define "freedom of individual". Citizenship was evaluated on the basis of both liberal and social theories with political, economic, and social developments, especially after the French Revolution. Here, the thought about the citizen was: "(Citizen) was in essence seen the problem of the reduction of class division and the integrating of ordinary people with management in all aspects of society. This aim was thought to require two exchanges by the state. One would be to establish a welfare state and the other to expand industrial self-management" (Miller et al., 1995: 457–459). At this point, in the transition from the modern period to the present day, one of the most controversial issues in the name of citizenship has been the policies of the "welfare state" and secondly the "conscious citizen" in the form produced by the welfare state. Here, it is important to evaluate the citizen depending on the welfare state.

It is certain that in the discussions on the welfare state, there are experiences regarding the connection between democracy and citizenship. With the expansion of other rights, citizenship came to the fore, including the right to vote in the 19th and 20th centuries. In this period, more than half of the adult population gained the rights that they needed to influence the decisions taken by the state administration, which they had to comply with in the context of laws and policies in practice. However, in this period of time, it is observed that a small part of the citizens spends their time in order to gain political influence in democratic countries, however, most of the citizens who are aware of their rights do not get involved in these issues at all (Dahl, 2018: 57–58). In other words, the citizen meeting social and economic conformism in the modern period took a passive attitude to affect the decisions taken about him as an important subject of the political system.

In the 1930s, the "state" was the sole responsible for determining the position of the citizen in the system as a political figure. However, within the framework of the spirit of the period, various ideological understandings occupied an important place in order to describe the citizen as a figure in political systems. Radical confrontation of citizens based on different thoughts coincides with this period. Various social movements such as *"front populaire"* (popular front), national socialism, fascist corporatism, new deal, and Scandinavian red-green (worker-farmer movement) emerged in Europe during this period. It is seen that each of these understandings gave rise to different citizen profiles "from the individual to the supersonal level, or from a more critical perspective". Although these differences lead to the ideological discussing of the citizen, it paves the way for its nutrition from different intellectual sources to raise awareness. While this was the case in the 1930s, a general view of citizenship gained importance through a process in which the state was fully legitimized and approved economically after the WWII, in the 1950s and 1960s. In these years, the state was considered as the sole tool of the argument that the economy and the market could be governed by politics. The dominant economic understanding of the period paved the way for the strengthening of the idea that "the nature of these connections can be managed politically by explaining the links between employment, investment, and the value of money" (Strath, 2011: 200).

Considering what happened after the Second World War in many dimensions, it is the main determinant of the process surviving to the present day. The rise of the facts of "social citizenship understanding" and "state intervention" after the War has been the main source of tension in the debates on freedom and equality regarding citizenship. As the aging population has increased and the death rates have decreased, the pension financial burden has put on the state increased significantly in this period. In addition, the decrease in the ratio of the working population within the general population has reduced the tax revenues of the state. So, due to the inequality between the balancing of the majority of the population that would finance the disease, retirement, and old age, some social and health cuts that voters would necessarily accept have emerged. Typical middle-class voters having recently formed have viewed the personal income tax deductions after a while and have not even see it as a problem in terms of citizen rights (Isin & Turner, 2009). However, it is not clear that this approach has received full support from all political segments in the West. For example, especially the right political tradition opposed the idea of "social rights" discussed above after the war. The reasons for the resistance of these right-wing political traditions are as follows: "These rights are (a) incompatible with (negative) demands of freedom or (empowerment-based) justice, (b) economically inefficient, and (c) opens the path to serfdom". It is claimed that the theses of the right political tradition against social rights have become irrational in the eyes of the public for a while. Especially against the social rights within the framework of Marshall's views, it is thought that the theses of the right political tradition would be "rightfully invalid against a citizenship-based welfare state" (Kymlicka and Norman, 2008: 189). Marshall's views really broke the views of the right politics at the citizenship point in the West until the economic crisis of the 1970s. However, in the following process, it was revealed that criticisms of the right politics towards the welfare state could be justified. The successive economic crisis periods such as inflation, deflation, and recession during the 1970s paved the way for the welfare state to be questioned by the state officials.

Leaving the above developments aside; the only concept where citizenship awareness based on welfare state can be addressed is "culture", which is considered as "a people's way of life". At this point, traditional and institutionalized views treated within of political culture after the 1950s and 1960s gave its place to new ones on the agenda. With the development of "new behavioral analysis techniques", it has been considered necessary to evaluate the political attitude analysis of some citizenship data in some Western democracies. The "civic culture model" formed in this context is classified as "participatory culture, subjects culture, and parochial culture". Thus, it is aimed to understand whether the public is a "participatory" political culture object as an economic and social being within the political culture (Heywood, 2012: 301). The break here on behalf of the welfare state was the recognition and identification of the citizen who knew and defended his/her interests.

In the period of 1968, a new process started to be observed, which included treating the citizen with an "individualist" incentive. The rhetoric carried out on freedom and equality in 1968 was described as "screams for liberation from the state or parental authority" in the name of citizenship. This rhetoric "hid behind the discourse of class struggle" with a focus on the United States and had the effect that the citizen now focuses on individual entity. This individual-oriented understanding was assessed on, "simultaneous modernity stories, such as clothing, culture, and education at that time – in which the citizen assumed responsibility for the formation of new communities against the collectivity of the welfare state and the nuclear family as a way of expressing himself" – (Strath, 2011: 203). This new perspective towards the citizen has been seen as the product of a development process in harmony with the spirit of the time. It is seen that the citizen is considered as an individual under the influence of the changing world rather than a problem of awareness.

The developments in this context show that the opinions preaching that citizenship should develop with an individual focus started to come to the fore after the World War II, while envisaged to form awareness of citizenship in many Western constitutions. The new constitutions made in this process tried to be formed the understandings of citizenship within the framework of "the idea that everyone equally benefits from the order" and "that ensures it is necessary to save people from misery and provide them with human living conditions". In particular, with the concept of "living humanly", individual-oriented "classical rights" started to be based on again (Kapani, 1993: 57). Within the framework of a new definition of citizenship, the emphasis on the formation of conscious individuals increased rather than a conscious society. However, the answers given to the question of how the individual is consciously put the society at the forefront. Bauman, in this sense, drew attention to the importance of the "social pressure" factor in the stage of forming a conscious individual. Bauman specifically expressed the relationship between the development of the concept of the elements of "freedom" and the "pressure" as follows:

"Every time we fail to 'personify' crime despite our enthusiastic pursuit, from social pressure; that is, we tend to speak of an inevitable consequence of the community's own entity, a natural necessity (when we do not intend to do something for it) or a repression resulting from a defective organized society (when we still hope to get rid of it).

No matter how one explains the feeling of oppression, the roots of this feeling always lie in the collision between their intentions (or what they experience as their own intent) and their action possibilities. Such a collision is supposed to be expected from a 'socially displaced' society, that almost everyone living in it is constantly subjected to the uncoordinated and often inconsistent demands and pressures and their mutually overlapping evaluations from a larger society that come from semi–autonomous functional sectors. Paradoxically society, thanks to its functional diversity, leaves the individual a lot of choices and makes it a truly 'free' individual, while the same society is responsible for the pressure experience on a large scale (2018: 71)".

Considering the above context, the social rights of citizens and their initiatives within the framework of these rights are important today. The processes related to the loss of liberty regarding citizenship are investigated by the courts according to the ideology of the existing sovereign states. While the state is decisive for some rights, the opinions about some rights on "the state must exist independently" are determinant to distinguish the present and modern understandings. For example, according to John Rawls, human rights should now be established apart from constitutional rights or liberal democratic citizenship. Rawls called them 'special class rights on vital issues'. For him, these rights have opened up a space for "individual freedom" today, unlike modern period on behalf of citizenship. These are; the right to be protected from slavery, mass killing, and genocide (Isin & Turner, 2009: 12). Although the presentation and publication of these rights contains certain specificities, it is not clear how citizens determine their situation against the state today. The issues dealt with in the "rights" dimension are still controversial. It was stated by authors such as Thomas Janoski that the issue is not over the citizenship title, but the multi-dimensionality of the issue, saying that there are issues that should be discussed in an "interdisciplinary" dimension. However these rights are related to the state of the citizen in front of the state, it is within the framework of the acquisition of basic rights in important works in the field of political thoughts and social sciences. Social movements towards rights are still carried out in the dimension of thoughts, and a ground where the issue of rights takes citizenship as a concept has not been established yet (1998).

At this point, Jürgen Habermas' view of the issue is also important in terms of demonstrating through which points the citizenship debates are addressed at present day. Habermas is quite liberal in human rights aspect of Rawls and has distance against his opinions on awareness of citizenship as well as he's liberal. Habermas voices a thought that expresses "emotional loyalty in a constitutional patriotism" against Rawls questionable and unclear understanding of citizenship about how it can be protected from all kinds of political and administrative rapes. Habermas thinks that "citizens of a state consider their nation as the greatest hope for a mature and sustainable democracy". However, the opinions of Habermas, who voiced the above thoughts against Rawls, also contain some problems according to James Donald. For Donald, the biggest problem of Habermas' views is that it reveals many uncertainties with problem areas such as "Can any set of institutional arrangements, regardless of how rational and fair, really instill into self-structures with a strict authority seen in *nation* and *public* claims? and Can it manage our loyalty or stimulate our desires?" (2008: 142–143). As can be seen, the issue from is controversial on which point or from which perspective the citizen can be treated within the framework of a conscious being and rights. Such discussions, which make it difficult to compromise on the subject, also make it difficult to draw the current position of the citizen.

It can be seen that today it is difficult to find an area where the citizen can be the subject of completely political discussions. Union strategies and approaches of worker's organization, which were discussed in many dimensions especially after the 1970s, caused various tensions. When gender-based problems were added to them, it was possible for even women to be considered as a problem area in citizenship discussions. The gender problem is an important area for citizenship to become a conscious being. It is important to reveal that "the gender dimension has its own political goals stated clearly, as a mobilizing category of identity" through civilization, even though ignored for much of the modern period. At this point, especially the bureaucratic strict attitude and certain patterns in the political sense were opened to discussion from the 1970s to the 1980s. In this process, some modern values were discussed with the concept of "flexibility" and also changed the axis of the idea of citizenship through production relations. In the citizenship debates, it was possible to deal with "individual" and "class" and "gender" differences in many dimensions (Strath, 2011: 208–209). In the new period, such specific areas ass race, gender, class, etc., which can be taken into a legal basis on a political and social basis by addressing citizenship, have been specialized. This has turned the political areas going beyond the citizenship framework into new paradoxical and grift problem areas in the intellectual and ideological context.

Besides the above developments, the economic recession in the 1980s worldwide and *monetarist*[12] politics as a result of this are important in the change of the citizenship debate. economic problems started critical debates covering many areas of social sciences through the welfare state, including the reconsideration of the citizen". At this point, the negative effects of the crisis in "public welfare principles" on the development of citizenship rights were used by right-wing politicians. Rights of citizens started to be questioned especially through *Thatcherism*[13], a spokesperson

---

12 Monetarism is "the economic opinion that argues that the main factor affecting the economy is monetary and monetary policies, and that monetary policy should be given great importance to improve economic balances by establishing a direct relationship between inflation and money supply. This understanding is also referred to as *"Friedmanism"* as pioneered by the major economic philosopher, Michael Friedman. Accordingly, the factors affecting production, employment, and prices in economic life should be evaluated through changes in money supply (Demir & Acar, 2002: 330).

13 Margaret Thatcher, who served as prime minister in Britain between 1979 and 1990, was accepted as the "loyal defender of national sovereignty" within the framework of the European Union on behalf of her own country. Thatcher is also regarded as an important new-right leader, who opposed the repression of "federalist" and transnational structures in the world over national states. Thatcher is one of the pioneers of the removal of market interventions and the development of the free market economy in the 1980s, particularly within the European Union (Dinan, 2005: 358–359). In this context, Thatcherism aimed at correcting "the growing concerns about social disintegration and weakening authority" of the economic crisis, accepted as a result of the failure of the Keynesian social democratic model in the 1970s. This phenomenon is defined the demolition of statism and the establishment of an alternative market through the new-right policies. The activities carried out within this framework are also seen as the defense of values such as freedom, choice, rights, and competition of neo-liberalism. This new-right understanding is

for new right-wing policies in particular of the British politics. This situation, read through new parameters on a global scale, indicates a fundamental change in the industrial societies of monetarist policies in the field of social policy. This change was perceived as the collapse of the reformist understanding in which the conscious citizen tried to be form in the period of social restructuring in the West after the WWII (Turner, 2008: 107). However, it is controversial how much criticism developed in the new right-wing axis and made from the welfare state is accepted on a social basis. Especially the people who still see themselves on the left say "social rights are necessary" for citizenship to exist and still defend the welfare state. This opinion reveals Marshall's ideas on "people can become full members of society and participate in common life only when their basic needs are met" (Kymlicka & Norman, 2008: 192). These ideas are the basis of the new citizenship concept constituted by the European Union's concept of "continental people", which transcends the national dimension and carries it to the international dimension. Jan-Werner Müller explained what this concept considered as a political idea means for the citizens:

> "What known as 'the European Union' since 1993 has gained political visibility, especially since it has put its political goals more sharply in focus. Under the effective leadership of Commission President Delors, the European integration has expanded towards both the common currency and a common project of Union citizenship (however, this was based on citizenship in the member states, and according to some researches, about two-thirds of the "European citizens" were completely unaware of the situation). Such economic and political deepening of the Union in this way was completed with the expectation that it would later expand towards new democratizing countries in the Central and Eastern Europe – or in the eyes of many observers, the Union was opened to competition in this way... As a result, what they described as the *de facto* constitution of Europe for a long time by the jurists increasingly seemed to follow Samuel Pufendorf's famous definition of the Holy Roman Empire: *simile monstro* – that is, an incomprehensible freak for ordinary citizens and also many bureaucrats and politicians probably (2012: 92–93)".

Although they are evaluated within quite different perspectives, the facts of democracy and democratization develop under the influence of post-era

---

described as *Reaganism* in the United States and *Thatcherism* in Great Britain by the leaders of the period (Heywood, 2012: 118).

and globalization discourses that strengthened after the mid-1990s. Aside from the European Union's discourse above "continental people", the Union is having different debates within itself. In the United States as the other side of the West, individual and society-based discussions are important without mentioning the intellectual and theoretical citizenship. In this context, the citizenship debates in the United States are based on the disputes "arising between libertarians and communitarians in social sciences". Looking at the concept of freedom and equality that marked the last quarter of the 20th century from a historical perspective, the "long debate between *Kantianists*[14] and *Hegelians*"[15] continues, changing. In

---

14 New Kantianism came to the fore with its opposition to irrational conceptions, fictional naturalism approaches, and positivism, highly influential in political philosophy between the 1870s and 1920s on political, social, and metaphysical issues. The expansion of natural sciences in a very generalized area, including social and political events, is criticized by the New Kantianists. The new Kantianists oppose "Kant's idea of the arrival of practical reason before theoretical philosophy" and in the monopolization of "sciences such as legislative sciences and history and human sciences". It is accepted that they are trying to strengthen the distinction between sciences. In this context, the new Kantianists emphasize the understanding of "the fact that science, ethics, and law exist as cultural products" rather than understanding events with "perceptional facts or self-observation" (Güçlü et al., 2008: 1595–1597). Here, the Kantianists, who paved the way for the discussion of the "perfect state" understanding in a "legal" dimension, drew on a moral framework in the field of public law and "law of states" over the concept of "cosmopolitan law". The Kantianists have an important place in the debates on the termination of "artificiality" in the effort to reconcile law and morality in the solution of the "state problem with the movements of nature" (Philonenko, 2003: 491–503). Some of the thinkers considered to be Kantian in the modern period are Helmholtz, Liebmann, Lange, Cohen, Cassirer, Rickert, Windelband, Natorp, and Ernst.

15 The thinkers defining themselves as Hegelian are producing ideas by referring to Hegel's views on many different subjects in many social, political, legal, and philosophical issues. Today, it is accepted that two understandings of Hegelism have developed. It is seen that they are trying only to defend Hegel's thoughts in the first one and to get a better understanding of Him. The aim here emerges as the continuation and development of the Hegel philosophy. This is called "Orthodox Hegelism". However, the owners of the second understanding basically accept Hegel's views. But they emphasize the need for restructuring the gaps in his thought. This understanding is called "Innovative Hegelism" or "Reformist Hegelism". Rather than the generalizations of Hegel, this

these discussions, strong determinations made to the free individual and political and social structure analyzes idealized through small communities are at the forefront. This concept facilitated the understanding of the American citizenship concept in global discussions. However, despite the universal emphasis of the European Union, the citizenship debates in Europe could not be detached from the history of the Continent. It is the general acceptance that the political philosophy in Europe is the result of the accumulation of three or four centuries after the Peace of Westphalia. Particularly, the culture of citizenship, which is especially nation and state oriented and inspired by the idea of "sovereign states that do not interfere with each other's internal affairs", is dominant in the Continent. Citizenship in this understanding first accepted the person as an entity equipped with secular guarantees based on the social one. However, this European view has started to erode in the face of "a general state logic reduced to guarantee private interests" in new global-based discussions (Strath, 2011: 213–214). At this point, the biggest intellectual coup has been on the understanding of the "state", which is evaluated through the nation provided by the integrity of the citizens. The blow gotten by globalization for the relationship of state and nation is described by Bauman as follows:

understanding attempts to verify themselves on the compatible and incompatible aspects of Hegel's thoughts with regard to modern science, especially against materialist, utilitarian, positivist, and naturalistic thoughts especially within the framework of religious science. This understanding has tried to find answers to current political, social, and philosophical debates (Güçlü et al., 2008: 654–655, 1594–1595). In the reflection of this in politics, it is defended the perspective of that "the state is the reality of concrete freedom". They try to develop a "universal" understanding from Hegel's philosophy of law, which evaluates the idea of understanding the state as a social expression of politics from an "ethical" perspective. It was stated by Marx that this point of view is an advanced understanding of state according to then. One hundred and fifty-two hundred years passed since these views of Marx. But it is the general acceptance that Hegel's debates on the "relationship between society and state in a hierarchical integration" are still current (Bourgeois, 2003: 359–368). The Hegelian thinkers in the modern period are Marx and Lukacs, Dilthey, Croce, Gentile, Wahl, Kojéve, Gabler, Craid, Bradley, Taggart, Strauss, and Erdmann, until a certain period of his life.

"Globalization means that the state's desire to continue its marriage with the nation, which is as solid and durable as a stone, or its influence over the nation is removed anymore. Extramarital flirting and even adultery incidents are both inevitable and permissible, and they are carried out with great sincerity and enthusiasm. (In order to meet the conditions set for admission to the 'free world' – first to the OECD and then to the European Union –, the governments of the Central European countries have opened their national assets to the global capital and removed all barriers to the flow of global finance.) The states that transfer most of their labor–and–capital intensive duties to the global markets need much less supply of patriotic enthusiasm. Even the feelings of patriotism, as the assets that nation–states guard with great jealousy, have been transferred to the market forces and reorganized by them to maximize the profits of the organizers of industries of the sports, entertainment, annual festival, and commemoration (2019: 39–40)".

As Bauman clearly emphasizes, it is seen that globalization is preparing the ground for the transformation of citizenship in the economic, political, and social aspects through a liberal-individualist approach. After a certain point, it is witnesses that the constitutions of the country, which dealt with citizenship within the framework of liberal-individualist understanding, are formed at the point of drawing the "legal" framework of a liberal-individualistic consciousness. According to this understanding, it is only evaluated through sample practices how to form a conscious citizen. As we have discussed in many parts of the text, the most obvious example at this point is the United States. The Constitution of the United States is one of the legal texts that discuss the most prominent features of liberal-individualist understanding with the "ten articles" added to the Constitution later. Moreover, in Great Britain, the situation was regulated according to the liberal-individualist understanding, without a constitutional structure, with the laws enacted the accepted "rights" of citizens. Although citizens have recently brought up constitutional demands of protection in Great Britain, the situation is still maintained within the framework of traditional processes and additionally with liberal-individualist approach. But *"what is the understanding of liberal-individualistic citizenship that is indispensable in the Anglo-American tradition and tends to spread to the rest of the world through globalization and what is it based on?"*. For Oldfield, the theoretical basis of the paradigm where this understanding prevails and the rights it covers are as follows:

"Rights" are the internal part of individuals; because individuals come before logically and morally both from society and from the state, which is obliged to ensure the safety and protection of individuals. These are "natural" or "human" rights. From the 17th century to the 20th century, the rights written, defended and fought for were basically civil, political, legal, and religious: freedoms of expression, assembly, and association; the right to vote and participate in political events; the right to protection from arbitrary arrest and fair trial; the right to worship as desired, without any civil or political deprivation to worship in the churches where the state control have not (2008: 95)".

In line with this approach, ordinary citizenship of the United States is seen as follows today: "It thinks that the country's form of administration is pluralist democracy in which the competing interest groups and the public in general determine public policy. The state is seen as a neutral area where the public discussions are made. While the elected representatives and appointed bureaucrats direct the demands of the public, they express it on the other hand (Carnoy, 2014: 27)". This approach is also the result of presenting the citizenship of the United States as an exemplary citizenship model to the world within the framework of multiculturalism. But today the understanding of *multiculturalism*[16] has many practical problems. According to sociologist Nathan Glazer, the multicultural approach used to emphasize the political and social structure in the United States seems to be collapsing in today's world conditions. The society in the United States is becoming more divided gradually. There is a growing discrimination against those who are the Hispanic origin in the country, and it is a paradoxical situation, proving itself in the conflicts with the

---

16 Multiculturalism came to the fore in the mid-1960s, with "the public debates in Canada, when grassroots activists, senior politicians, and liberal thinkers faced the same problem". In the process that took place in the Quebec region in Canada and reached the discussions of leaving the country politically, the "civil and cultural demands of rights" of firstly the indigenous people, then the nationalist community, and finally the immigrants who came to the region later developed the subject. Today, the phenomenon is used to "survive discrimination based on ethnic, racist, religious or national criteria; briefly, to emphasize a 'social image' that is formed regardless of cultural difference". (See more for a detailed information: Baumann, Gerd (2016), "Çok–Kültürlülük (Multiculturalism)", Trans. Mehmet Karataş, **Sosyal Bilimler Ansiklopedisi** 'İkinci Kitap/A–K', Edit. Adam Kuper–Jessica Kuper, Adres Yayınları, Ankara, ss. 217–223).

neighboring Mexico. This situation is seen in many conflicts caused by the economic and political problems in the United States. The last example on the subject in the country is that the *"Clash of Civilizations"* debates, which are thought of being existed between political Islam and the West, are increasing day by day (Isin & Turner, 2009: 11). Even these problem areas in the United States reveal the difficulties of liberal-individualist understanding, treated with globalization, and of the citizenship and citizenship awareness in reaching social common points.

The theoretical basis of liberal-individualism is based on Jeremy Bentham (1748–1832) and James Mill (1773–1836). At this point, it is envisaged that today's liberal-individualist thought is connected to the idea of *"utilitarianism"*[17] in the name of the happiness of the society. The notion of *"pluralism"*,[18] which is frequently discussed today, becomes politicized through multiculturalism in today's citizenship debate. The pluralist models tried to be explained in particular with the above facts and proposed for social

---

17 Utilitarianism, considered as a moral doctrine of philosophy, claims that "the 'accuracy' of an activity, policy or institution can be evidenced by the tendency to increase happiness. This claim is based on the assumption that individuals are motivated by self-interests and that these interests can be defined as the desire for pleasure or happiness and the desire to avoid pain and unhappiness". In this understanding, individuals choose "the way promising the greatest pleasure" based on their pleasure and pain. At this point, utilitarian thinkers believe that pleasure and pain can measure "benefit". So, people aim for the greatest pleasure, the lowest pain. The opinions of Jeremy Bentham on this subject were formulated as "the greatest benefit for the greatest number of people". Utilitarianism has reached today by being accepted as a classical liberal theory (Heywood, 2012: 129–130).

18 In a broad sense, pluralism is "believing and connecting to diversity and differences – the entity of many things". When considered in a normative manner, pluralism is a concept that "diversity and differences are healthy on its own" and "usually ensures individual freedom" (Heywood, 2012: 251). The phenomenon was used in the framework of political science to emphasize social and political acceptances within the framework of empirical studies in the United States of America in the 1960s. Particularly, it politically defines Robert Dahl's concept of "the distribution of political power among competitive interest groups". Pluralism is generally accepted as a phenomenon that maintains its place in political debates in terms of the ability of different groups in the society to protect their interests (Marshall, 1999: 122).

peace are still popular. However, the *social corporatism*[19] approach developed against these pluralist insights claims that today's liberal democratic systems have great difficulty in post-modern societies. Social corporatism is one of the many theories that emerge due to the insufficiency of pluralist understandings against authoritarian-totalitarian governments that may have right or left origins. This understanding sees the "humane but powerful state decision making mechanism" as an imperative in today's complex world conditions. Social corporatism draws attention to some of the problems of the idea of "(more) democracy" in the name of societies including multiculturalism. According to this understanding, political systems go to "mobocracy" after a while under the name of democracy. In this case, it carries the risk of leading to an understanding that sees society only as a democratic "apparatus". The basic logic in such insights is constructed as "a rational state, led by right-thinking leaders, is a logical way of managing the country's economy, foreign policy, and social policy for citizens' own good". The main claim of social corporatism here is that today's liberal democratic and political structures are not on the side of democracy and citizens who are democratically empowered by social and political rights, and their main goal is to save the system from the "boundaries on the economic role of the state" (Carnoy, 2014: 311). Therefore, according to social corporatism, liberal representative democratic systems are the main reason why citizens are atomized today. For them, a conscious and

---

19 This fact emphasizes "a type of society that is driven by the interests of organizations in the form of large-scale corporations, in the processes of economic, social, and political decision-making". Professional organizations, corporate groups, unions, and pressure groups, acting in the interests of the groups of people acting jointly, are considered within this framework. In particular, some of the social scientists examined the effects of the multinational corporations that emerged in the 20th century on the economy, their effects on the states, and especially the social dimensions of their influences on democratic processes in the countries through the entity of a corporatist relationship. The discussion of the working class as a dimension of social corporatism through union movements came to the agenda after 1945. Social corporatism is addressed as a subject "related to political and industrial conflicts seen in capitalist societies", and it is still an important area of discussion on these issues (Marshall, 1999: 429–430).

solidarity citizen as a social being is possible only in a state that can be formed by revising liberal democratic systems.

Such conceptions as 'social corporatism' that open the Western liberal democratic political structures to discuss evaluate social and political rights for the future of society in the name of citizenship. In the post-modern period, it is normal for such understandings to come to the agenda when citizens or citizenship reach a certain level of consciousness. Because it is accepted as normal to consider citizenship awareness through a certain welfare and social solidarity that can be achieved especially at economic points. It is the result of an important process that citizenship awareness in the Western norms turns itself into an object of development with political, social, legal, and eventually, economic facts. After WWII, the Western states assumed great responsibilities in such subjects as work, health, nutrition, housing, retirement, etc. that first cover the individual and then the whole society. It is a fact that these states pave the way for a significant accumulation in the world in terms of production and consumption at an unprecedented level. This leads to a more organized and homogeneous understanding of citizenship in the West. So, it is a reality that an organized society is formed in order to form citizenship awareness in the West in a significant part of the modern period. In the formation of today's citizen, the modern Western systems "succeed in joining the reconciliation and balance together that pleases the economic, social, and political parties at a minimum level". This process in the West also constitutes an important stage for the formation of a conscious citizen on a social basis (Özalp, 2009: https://www.academia.edu/1352472/Yoksulluk_Yoksunluk_Yurtta%C5%9Fl%C4%B1k_Sosyal_Hak_s%C4%B1zl%C4%B1k_lar%C4%B1_Politik_D%C3%BC%C5%9F%C3%BCnmek, s. 278). However, the Western modern democracies, which are decisive for the formation of this awareness on behalf of the citizen, also encounter serious political, social, and economic problems. Imbalances in the speeds of social and economic development in the state systems of the Western countries lead to discussions of the "democracy gap" as a general acceptance occasionally. This situation gives rise to critical perspectives in the West about "deterioration of trust between the public and politicians and the standards of behavior of politicians". This has always been one of the most important issues that keep the agenda in the West. In today's world, there are debates about the advanced and highly knowledgeable citizen profile as a social entity to join the system as a whole. This paves the way for how the democracy deficit can be reduced today and more voices between the politicians and the public at least to understand each other (Joyce, 1999).

Today, the *communote* approach, which deals the citizen with an important subject of the political system and the society with a more solidarity dimension, becomes in the foreground. This understanding is one of the popular understandings in the sense of consciousness of community building. According to the *communote* understanding, the effect of the unity of the groups close to each other in the society can be important in forming citizenship awareness. At the point of the *communote* debates, some political thinkers consider models in the meaning of "political autonomy". These thinkers emphasize the strengthening of communities' perception of "equality" and the importance of a multi-dimensional approach to "justice". It is accepted that economic inequalities can arise in the *communote* thought within the framework of the understanding of forming political community. However, this is not a serious mistake considering the large picture of the society. Because it is possible that it may have controversial results at a point that makes social benefits in the distribution of riches. Despite this assumption, the *communote* understanding contains some uncertainties as you see. The attitude of the *communote* approach especially at the point of economic inequalities raises serious question marks as it may have negative consequences within the framework of the rights of today's citizens (de Lara, 2003: 517). When political autonomy is taken together with equality, it is a reality that it presents some problems regarding the individual's socio-economic freedom as a citizen. In this context, Richard Sennett's thoughts can provide a better understanding of the problematic areas at the point of *communote* understanding in order to form conscious citizens:

> "One of the reasons why autonomy... causes strong emotions is that people believe that autonomy means freedom. A worker in Boston had told me: 'As long as they can push you in, you're nothing'. Ordinary people have this in mind: Controlling the flow of influence provides the chance to self-control rather than pleasure of dominating. Autonomy builds a wall against the outside world; once a person takes shelter, he can live as he wants (2017: 135)".

Another discussion about the formation of citizenship consciousness is within the framework of the concept of *"social justice"*[20]. The discussions on the "universality" of this phenomenon are concentrated on the *"heterogeneity"* point, based on the fact that societies are composed of equal individuals. The discussing of the phenomenon includes associations with many eclectic concepts as it is carried out both in the context of universal

---

20 Social justice, which is seen as one of the most important concepts in citizenship discussions, is an important issue to understand. In this sense, opinions on the concept of social justice are reported in many fields of social sciences. Here, the general acceptance is that "justice is a moral standard at the center of social life". So, justice plays an important role in social theory and understanding of social action in general. While justice can be dealt with in different dimensions in legal, political, and economic terms, there are some interpretations that these are related to each other. Because it is accepted that there is a serious relationship between punishment and its social consequences. In this sense, the fact that the wrong behaviors within the framework of social benefit do not go unpunished is considered as an important justice problem. As a dimension of mutual relationship, an agreement was reached on the "divisive justice, namely the principle of fair distribution, which envisages the one-way distribution of rights, obligations or similar things". When dealing with the dimension of equality, social justice emerges at the point of "the distribution of awards complies with normative expectations that prevents the sense of injustice". At this point, when the welfare, family, education, and social gains are taken into consideration, the activities of modern state structures towards individuals are important. It is observed that there is still no standard emerging in the dimension of "how to apply various principles of justice in practice as well as how to determine the deserving and performance factors". It is a matter of debate today that solving of these problems fully can lead a "universal" understanding at the point of social justice. Because ordinary citizens here are characterized as "tending to unite analytically contradictory principles of social justice, to resolve the dilemmas of justice by making subjective decisions, and to move from one norm to another without explicitly expressing it". However, it is difficult to establish a common literature for the acquisition of social justice "in fairness" in a social dimension that covers all societies. These issues have been discussed in a wide range from Karl Marx to John Rawls and from socialism to various liberal theories, and they are still being debated. However, it is a fact that a consensus is still being tried to solve the problems of social justice (For detailed discussions on this issue, see; Marshall, Gordon (1999), **Sosyoloji Sözlüğü** (Sociology Dictionary), Trans. Osman Akınhay–Derya Kömürcü, Bilim ve Sanat Yayınları, Ankara, pp. 735–740).

justice and a heterogenized society. This raises some questions about the results of discussions on citizen awareness raising in the framework of social justice. So, there are some problems in the use of the concepts formed for the solution of political problems especially in the post-modern period. Meaningful changes in certain frameworks related to the facts including political solution suggestions are in mention. Thus, a situation arises that the discussions about producing political solutions cannot be handled on a common ground. In this context, the understanding of social justice also contains some troublesome ideas. Summarizing these troubles, Harvey defines social justice as an inevitable understanding "to turn into deconstruction in a way that can make every kind of sense, except for the meanings that individuals or groups with different identities and functions find appropriate at giving in pragmatic, instrumental, emotional, political or ideological for a moment" (2001: 182).

The concepts of society and community, which are always seen as rivals or even opposites in the discussions of political philosophy, appear as part of a common element, as they have never been in the past. At this point, the concepts of society and community are an important problem area in discussing today's social and economic doctrines within the theory of politics. However, the belief that community formations lead to instability in modern imaginations in the formation of society has been broken at certain points today. It is important to discuss the conflict between these concepts within a theoretical framework. Today, with the phenomenon of "balance society" which is opened to new discussion, the understanding that the society and the community can be together is tried to be discussed (Pasquino, 2003: 522). Especially in neo-liberalism, it is seen that political facts are tried to be revised through many new debates. Because, within the framework of globalization, the effort to form a new citizen according to neo-liberal understanding has been on the agenda since the last quarter of the 20th century. The fact that this understanding constitutes a new theoretical citizenship theory is explained by Lemke as follows by the citation of Balibar:

> "... As 'entrepreneur' individuals in every aspect of life, the subjects are fully responsible for their own well-being, and (in this process) citizenship is reduced to the success of this entrepreneurship. Neo-liberal subjects are controlled *by* their liberty – the reason is not simply that freedom within an order

of domination can be the means of this domination, but rather neo-liberalism evaluates the consequences of this freedom in terms of moralization. This means: the withdrawal of the state from certain areas and the privatization of certain functions of the state does not mean the fragmentation of management, rather it establishes a management technique; in fact, it is the signature technique of neo-liberal governance, so that intellectual economic action that spreads to the society replaces the open state rule or provision. Neoliberalism imposes the regulatory power of the state on 'responsible', 'rational' individuals, [its aim] is to encourage individuals to give their lives a specific entrepreneurial form (2016: 119)".

The factor that strengthens the determinism of neo-liberalism for the post-modern period in the functioning of this process is neo-conservatism (conservative, neocon). Neo-conservatism adopts the empowerment of the state before society for the future of the traditional economic order and the sustainability of capitalism. According to neo-conservatism, it is certain that the perception of citizens also changes due to the changing economic and political nature of states. This view shows that the economic relations between home prices, savings, investments, and retirement make it necessary to evaluate the perception of citizenship of the Western governments at the new point of conservatism. For instance, individuals sell pension funds to buy property, such as home, and this leads to unusual price increases. Individual savings are still at a very low level, and the young population cannot acquire property despite low interest rates. Homelessness gradually rises in the society and becomes not only an economic problem but an ethical problem. Neo-conservatism links these to the politics of useless citizenship in the modern period. According to them, the economic principles (such as high personal tax, sufficient retirement income, welfare security) of citizenship, which was formed by Keynes in the midst of 20th century are now subject to wear. The social citizenship of modern democratic states is eroded accordingly. As a result, privatizations are made in the public. For this idea, the subject is that simple. But the source of current social and economic problems is the lack of current policies implemented by the governments, rather than systemic erosion and social change in the European Union and the United States. In addition, there are countries that see capitalism as the only reason for the development of countries today. For example, partial-authoritarian regimes such as Russia agree with this idea. However, in such countries, because the state establishes pressure policies on domination of the entire civil society, problems such as not being able to solve social problems by non-state actors arise. This prevents integrative organizations on behalf of the state-society in order for citizenship to show common solidarity against economic problems. Thus, the problems of citizens increase even more (Isin & Turner, 2009: 10). Today, rather than forming rights of citizens or a conscious citizen, an unprecedented influence and determination of the state and/or international collective organizations emerge. These negative developments, according to some authors, cause the "return theories" to come to the fore in terms of the position of the citizen in the modern period. Jan-Werner Müller, one of those who claims that political systems are far behind the modern period today, explains this fact as follows:

"(Today) what's called 'social integration' quite abstractly turns into a problem or in a slight word, a challenge for many different reasons and in different ways, and beyond these countries: As in the European Union, 'regional integration' is not the same as 'integration' of immigrants and minorities. There is a widespread belief that globalization strengthens the need for reconfiguration of collective identities, what is often referred to as the 'sense of belonging', in political, legal, and also emotional. Sovereignty was 'worn out' and citizenship was 'shattered' as said by a scientist... (According to an observation made in the United States) – that the national borders invoked anxiety about what it means to belong because it is ideological and thus controversial and permeable – we can say that it is correct for many countries. Maybe the whole world turns into America; having expressed in a less dramatic (and undoubtedly less threatening for somebodies), it almost everywhere becomes difficult to conceptualize both individual and collective 'belonging'; the citizenship bond becomes questionable (2012: 19)".

Today's change of the position of citizenship in the defense of social equality and interests, which appears to cause a serious confusion when given through the examples of global society and some countries, is evaluated by many different perspectives. In this sense, Heywood's idea of social change, which he sees in the context of globalization that is relatively positive and class conscious disappears as well as positive, gives us an interesting perspective:

"As a result of the striking trend towards social equality associated with mass education, increased wealth and consumerism, the narrowing of the traditional working class has led to the development of societies, two-thirds of which are relatively prosperous, at the rate of 'two-thirds and one-thirds'. J.K. Galbraith emphasized that this trend marks the emergence of modern 'satisfied majority' societies of which material wealth and economic security encourage political conservatism, at least among those who are politically active. In this process, the debate about the social inequality and the nature of poverty in modern societies has shifted away from concerns about the working class instead of those that are widely but controversially described as sub-classes. In addition to the poverty (lack of material requirements) understood traditionally, the sub-class suffers from social exclusion that emerges as cultural, educational, and social barriers to meaningful participation in the economy and society (2013: 179)".

Heywood's ideas about the social situation in the global era are important for citizenship. In parallel with this perspective, the effects of the globalization process on the citizens show similarities with the Marshallist approach in certain aspects. The most important similarity is the "universal" perspective towards the citizen in the early periods of the modern period. Because, citizenship debates no longer include not only people who share the same nationality and considered to be settled, but also contain new debates emerging through the position and situation of individuals coming to the country through immigration. At this point, the claims start to be voiced that the assumption "that almost all of the people share the same nationality, their parents are born in a certain country where they are born, and that they have to settle permanently in there" will not be able to contribute to the solution of current citizenship problems. According to these allegations, the position of immigrants in their new countries brought the argument in a debatable point that one of the nation-state-based depictions towards the citizen "to be considered as a group, each of which is accustomed to his country, connected to its culture by an oldest contract, and influenced his political destiny," on behalf of the Western states. In this case, the question of the extent to which "the rights or duties accepted as constituting the human subject reflects the different cultural preferences that seem to be universal and evaluated within the framework of general citizenship in the West" (Poggi, 2011: 50–51). This finding is controversial for citizenship in order to explain current problems. However, this problem area paves the way for discussion of all the solutions that the Western political systems, as an example to the world through immigration throughout the modern period, in the citizenship dimension.

Today, the Western developed nation states promote diasporic policies among immigrants and former citizens. These states strive to form not only a source of political support for projects within the diaspora, but also a source of networks, skills, and competencies that can be used to improve the stance of a state. This situation results in the execution of processes, carried out on some of the diasporic wide societies in a global world, at the project dimension. The outstanding examples of diasporas used at this point stand out as Indian, Chinese, and Jewish communities. The Western countries are used to accept their diaspora (new life environments) as their "homeland" to develop their civic loyalty and they are trying to accelerate their adaptation to the Western societies (Benhabib, 2009: 23). This is proof by some authors that some developed Western countries consider the immigrant citizens within the framework of a "single authentic" "national identity". From this point of view, the Western states tend to see immigrants only and only as "human" within the framework of a "political identity". This situation is fed with an understanding of citizenship that is constantly evaluated within the framework of "political belonging". Thus, the flow of immigrants to the developed Western countries is increasing. On the other hand, systematic questioning of nation-state structures increases gradually that should be seen as the result of an anomaly though. This situation causes the nation-states to be treated as a "political community unit" at the international level (Theodorakis, 2014: 38). This causes a serious paradox. Because the acceptance of the nation-state as a structural political unit has raised the question of how nation-state structures can contribute to the adaptation of citizens to countries as a conscious entity historically and hierarchically.

At this point, it is important to examine the current activities of global united structures of state such as the European Union, which we mentioned earlier. Because, it is thought that the European Union (with its historical dilemmas) may play some critical roles in subjects such as citizenship considered as a conscious entity and social adaptation of individuals. On this matter, Müller said:

> "The EU can provide a way to escape the logic of substituting a passion with another passion, an absolute loyalty with another absolute loyalty, and a political identity with another identity. (However) the EU should avoid substitutional (or rerouting) strategies in which national passions are replaced by "European passions" and devotion is redirected towards a European nation or constitution. This would seem to indicate a relativization strategy that somehow weakens passion completely and leads patriotism from a hostile relationship to a rational

"success" –and forms a *parvenu* European "ghost" that tries to shift the subject thoroughly from its troubled past (2012: 134)".

What is brought forward at this point is the citizen-oriented "spatial imagination" approach that the European Union puts forward as a political community proposal. This understanding has a citizenship standard that includes citizens within the Union. Here, it is focused on citizenship through the "claim". This claim is "the right of European citizenship to vote and participate in the municipal elections of the states linked to the European Union". The problematic situation for the European Union citizenship starts here. Because the answer to the question about what rights and responsibilities the citizen has beyond the local dimension in terms of rights and responsibilities is ambiguous. In particular, the place of the rights that can raise citizenship awareness in the Union has not been fully clarified. The key problem area at this point is shown as "while state limitation of citizenship is determined as wrong..." still not being able to answer "the question of whether it would make sense to limit citizenship regionally" (Dobson, 2011: 260–261). The situation that Dobson puts forward within this framework is that the liberal democratic systems have many deficiencies on behalf of the citizen on the basis of the European example. Dobson says that he has serious doubts about how much more liberal democratic governments can continue to be effective in the name of the post-modern era. In addition to Dobson's views, Dahrendorf's following findings are important for the paradoxical effects of liberal democracies on citizens' understanding of rights and responsibilities:

"I understand the (appeal) of relying on the referendum democracy in the era of political inconsistencies that the parliamentary system no longer functions in the usual way... There are cases when referendums are mandatory; e.g., during the construction of a constitution. However, in this case it is necessary to be protected from romance. The public's response should be a vote on the content of the constitution, rather than the instant popularity of politicians, even if it is applied on the public to make a decision on the constitution. Since the popularity, public influence, and market research become an obsession in the communities in which we live in the 21st century, the referendum is in danger of being included in a truly undemocratic scheme. In this 'Demos' hunt, I prefer tools that encourage, motivate, and guarantee public negotiation. This task is paradoxically best done by 'test and evaluation groups' in which at least 'representative' people discuss the problems in detail. Here is the problem of representation. This is not a marginal problem, because the future of a country cannot be determined by a small drilling made according to market research tools and criteria (2015: 84)".

It is argued that the main reason why modern societies are atomized today, whether in Europe or in the world, is still the desire of the states to be kept unchanged without changing, among the discussions carried at the present day. According to these debates, there are many ways to enable individuals to share political projects of states. Only these pathways need to be developed or transformed. At this point, reconciliation of republican and liberal ideas is considered an important way. In general, citizens can be gained with a more liberal attitude influenced by the liberal perspective, with a view that already exists in the republican tradition, and it can be considered more socialist. This is a foresight that citizen's "participation in all levels of public life through a strong decentralization" can increase the acceptability of political life. Within the framework of these two understanding common points, it is thought that it is possible to move the subjects and problems related to the general interest of the society to the areas where all citizens can be discussed. Thus, it is claimed that it can solve an important social awareness problem for the citizens. In this sense, it is accepted that the citizen's "participation in all levels of public life" can ensure the solution of a significant problem area for a conscious citizen formation from Machiavelli to Skinner (Audier, 2006: 123–124).

Within the framework of different opinions and solution suggestions, citizenship rights and citizenship as an equal being are today reevaluated. The future of citizenship is also discussed in practical and theoretical terms, with different dimensions and different political perspectives. It is seen that the interest groups that emerge as a total of "post-modern individuals", which are the result of the activities of forming a stable "political awareness of community" today, are a determinant element in the citizenship debate. It is certain that the interest groups today have a dimension of the economic, social, and cultural structure as an element of social balance. It is understood that a new social structure formed in this sense can play important functions with positive and negative aspects for the establishment, sustainability, and acceptance of legitimacy of today's stable societies. At this point, citizenship is a necessary phenomenon for the society to be composed of individuals who are both determinative and legally and administratively familiar with the rights and responsibilities of the political community. For this reason, citizenship will be a key to the operation of the political systems that emerge for the continuation of the "new" society, which will be formed by conscious individuals who are seen with their rights and responsibilities.

Conclusion and Evaluation

Citizenship, as the subject of serious discussions since the Ancient Greek, continues to be one of the main topics in the discussions about the ruling-ruled relations of human beings in the modern age or the post-modern age in when we are. The concept was produced in the West and used in the West for centuries as an important argument for the struggle of individuals in modern societies in the name of "freedom" and "equality" as a result of the legal and political transformation gone through in the West. Citizenship is also an important phenomenon that the Western civilization insists on in a significant part of the modern period to distinguish them from traditional and non-Western societies. In this context, citizenship emerges as one of the important areas of discussion at the solution point for political systems to be historically and theoretically "stable" structures in the Western societies.

The theoretical and historical debates in the Western world within the framework of both political, social and economic development processes and the history of the ancient and modern Western political thoughts are the main determinants of the periodic changes and transformations of citizenship.

Citizenship in its practical process is presented as a result of an important combination of political and social understanding in the Greek city-states in the ancient times and then in Rome. Especially the idea of "universal citizenship" based on rights and responsibilities, which is accepted to be the product of these two political structures, has been brought to the agenda in order to determine the place and position of the individual against the state in the name of social "stability". At this point, the human being tried to be defined as "citizen" is constructed on the basis of having some rights as a free and equal individual within its political and social structure. In this fiction, the citizen is described as a "political entity" who has "responsibilities" towards the state in which they live, and can also be "determinant" for the future of that state. In these understandings, the citizen is seen as a figure tried to be shaped in this direction at least. Depending on the above understanding; although citizenship is evaluated in terms of being "aristocratic" and "elected" in both Ancient Greek and Rome, the first examples discussed in the modern period are these two political systems. These two traditions, in which the philosophical dimension of "civic virtue" and the practical sense of "patriotism" are at the forefront, draw attention as the most focused theoretical understanding in today's citizenship discussions. The power of these two traditions has been so decisive that; especially in the period from Rome to the modern period, a unique model of citizenship that rivals these traditions in the name of the freedom and equality of the individual in European political and social history has not been produced. Even though one thousand five hundred years passed since the collapse of the Ancient Greek and a thousand years after the collapse of Rome, these traditions were tried to be imitated in the Renaissance city-state models as examples in terms of politics, social, and legal aspects. Especially in the Italian city-states, the emphasis on Rome is certain intellectually and practically.

Particularly the main reason why Rome's understanding of citizenship comes to the fore is that the administrative system formed by the Church Fathers and shaped by the Church bureaucracy is focused on the *"solidarity"* rather than the basic understanding of Christianity that shaped the Western world in the Middle Ages. The citizen, defined within the framework of this understanding, emerges as a *"disciple fused within the community"* within the framework of the limitations of the *"divine"* understanding that determines social rights, responsibilities, and duties. In the Middle Ages, the citizen was regarded as a silent entity with only "responsibilities" in terms of the ruling-ruled relations, since religious authority was the only dominant figure in the Western world for a long time. Renaissance played an important role in questioning this understanding. The citizen having historically been politically, philosophically, and economically important in taking its share from all the changes in the West has reached the secular and modern world through an individual connected to the city, starting from the Renaissance, with developments such as the Reform and the Industrial Revolution. However, what is certain is that citizenship has reached in the modern period with the serious intellectual influence of the Ancient Greek and Roman conceptions. The Enlightenment writers and thinkers tried to redefine citizenship both politically and socially through the parameters of the Ancient Greek and Rome.

In fact, citizenship, apart from all the ideological and intellectual debates determining the Enlightenment and the next period from time to time, became a determining element in the treating of the modern individual in terms of freedom and equality (Çelik, 2012).

At the end of its adventure in the West through the above discussion, the citizen can be said to be a product of the great transformations in the political and social dimensions, which took place in the modern period first in England and then in France. Citizenship evolves into an entity addressed through constitutionally provided rights, especially within the democratic governments and trends in the West. In this development process, it is accepted that the citizen reaches a "consciousness" in a modern sense in order to obtain legal and economic rights first and then to protect them through the struggles for the equality and freedom of individuals. Thanks to the "citizenship consciousness", which is accepted to be formed in this way, first the modern and then the current citizen exists with constitutional interpretations and definitions. In addition to its legal and political dimensions, today's citizen becomes a phenomenon that is closely related to the socially assigned role as an individual and has some social habits.

The historical process shows that the individual as a political, social or economic entity is the determinant of states at certain points. This at times becomes more determinant element in the West. The social evolution of the West shows that political authorities have to care about individuals from time to time in order to become a stable ruling device. State authorities resort to citizens and citizenship relations sometimes through religion for the continuation of the political system and sometimes through nation consciousness to provide legitimacy in order to have longer power in today's modern democracies. The key point here is that political systems seem to strive to show the individual as part of that formation. However, modern democracies are seen more theoretically and practically in terms of the construction of the citizen and the effort to transform the built-citizen into a political, social, and legal entity to accept it. Its main reason can be read as increasing the loyalty of the individual in the modern period to the state through citizenship in the economic and political activity at the point of maintaining the political system.

This request for loyalty is operated on different parameters when compared to the pre-modern era. However, the fact that the governments of those in power are stable and they can be regarded as legitimate is parallel to what they give to the citizen is the most important feature that distinguishes modern authorities from pre-modern authorities. Some important democracies in the West are seen that they understood that certain codes are essential for the happiness and welfare of the society since the 19th century. At this point, it is important to note that the important thing is to reach a consensus on the continuation of the political union between the state and the citizen. This situation emerges as a vital situation to ensure whether the national unity is a social consciousness issue for the citizens or not. This leads to be treated the citizenship discussions of modern period within the framework of first "popular sovereignty" and then "nation-state".

The level of consciousness formed for citizens is an important source of reference in order to determine the integrity of a nation as a political, social, and economic entity, firstly at the individual and then collective point, especially in the debates on freedom. Here the citizenship awareness, as an indicator of development and social welfare, comes to the fore in the name of Western indicators. Particularly, the measurability of consumption habits within the framework of today's conformism and the future political and social points of the society should be determined. This has now become an important parameter for measuring citizenship awareness. Although the framework of political and social rights can be determined by states, the data that can contain important clues in order to determine how the citizen should be defined with his rights and responsibilities changes every day. In this sense, it is very important to understand that citizenship emerges as a conscious entity with its rights and responsibilities at the economic point, especially according to today's indicators. If the citizen becomes a being who can be measured his level of consciousness, it seems more possible to predict the actions of the individual in legal, political, social, and economic aspects, and most importantly, to be satisfied. The efforts of the modern period towards the standardization of citizen-state relations are important at this point, but the discussions reveal that they are insufficient today. Today, the debates in this context emphasize that citizenship is one of the indispensable elements for the continuation of the organized structures that can provide political integrity, even if non-state structures are sometimes mentioned. With various alternatives, the subject goes beyond the discourse of freedom and equality.

The modern state, which started to be discussed in the post-modern period, or the nation-state, which is its most applied model today, is seen as the only organization that can make the citizen a conscious entity for two hundred years. Currently, it is the only structural institution that is ready legally, educationally, politically, and economically for the formation of conscious citizens. Leaving aside the ideological and bureaucratic preferences of different nation-states, the only practical device for determining the citizen, as an example of a concrete political structure, is still the nation-state today. All discussions on behalf of citizenship, whether immigrants, identity, or human rights, are conducted today through nation-states. According to the above general framework, it is seen that satisfactory results of citizenship awareness can be achieved through its legal, political, and economic reformation. For this reason, it is clear that all solution proposals on this issue can be carried out through the nation-state until new and concrete political structures that can form a citizenship awareness are revealed.

In the process of the formation of citizenship and citizenship consciousness in the modern period, it is seen that we are confronted with a mixture of concepts, which is first introduced by the Ancient Greek and Roman and then the Age of Enlightenment, as we emphasized before. However, it is seen that the developments affecting our day in terms of the content of citizenship have taken place in the last seventy-eighty years. Especially with the second quarter of the 20th century, it is a fact that there were important conceptual transformations towards citizenship in sociology science and developments that clarify serious rights and responsibilities in the legal dimension. At this point, the concept of "social rights", introduced by Thomas H. Marshall and enables modern period citizenship to be evaluated on the social welfare state, should be understood well. The basic concept of the theoretical and practical areas of politics, citizenship, and the discussions on the development of citizenship consciousness through this concept are social rights. These social rights determine the status and position of the citizen as a social, political, and economic entity in the Western and other countries that call themselves democratic. The obligations that Marshall puts forward and imposes on the state in treating citizens as equal and free entities in modern societies are still debated. However, the acceptance and operation of these rights are important in the Western norms to ensure that a human figure is shown as an example to other nations.

Today, the general acceptance is that Marshall's social rights in the Western societies, which are accepted as modern but homogeneous, are evaluated with their political and economic consequences that aim to make the citizen a free and equal individual, and this shows a positive historical development. However, the intense immigration towards the Western states from other parts of the world for the last thirty years led to the discussion of the citizen figure empowered with national consciousness together with the homogeneous and modern education processes of Marshall in the industrialized Western societies. While this situation forced the Western nation-states to transform towards heterogeneous social structures at national, religious, and cultural points, the discussions in the dimension of Marshallist social rights weakened and the discussions on freedom and equality in the dimension of political rights intensified. Especially the debates experienced over such facts as identity, multiculturalism, social corporatism, republicanism, neo-liberal/conservatism, etc. eroded the modern era understanding of the achievements of the citizen as a conscious being against the state through economic prosperity that concerns the whole society.

The beliefs that the individual is atomized for different reasons in urban life and that social equality cannot be achieved at any point without providing individual economic freedom paradoxically retard the issue of citizenship and the discussions related to it. In this context, post-modern thought patterns and currents that concern the individual as a cultural entity rather than a conscious social entity are quite popular. In addition, the fact that critical thinking in the post-modern period becomes the dominant paradigms of today causes citizenship to turn into a phenomenon that includes various anomalies. The "chaos" situation experienced in relation to the content of many phenomena is also experienced in the name of "citizenship", and within this framework, it becomes very difficult to discuss citizenship within general and universal norms. The intellectual basis through "political equality" based on the ancient ideas formed in the name of citizenship and "social and economic equality" established in the modern sense has difficulty in solving today's problems. It is a great dilemma that the citizenship awareness trying to be formed through ancient and modern conceptions can be evaluated over which understandings of equality and freedom today. As in many important facts, the future of citizenship will also be determined by time and people's thoughts.

References

Arena, Valentina (2016), "Popular Sovereignty in the Late Roman Republic", Edited by Richard Bourke-Quentin Skinner, **Popular Sovereignty in Historical Perspective**, Cambridge University Press, Cambridge, pp. 73–95.

Asen, Robert (2004), "A Discourse Theory of Citizenship", **Quarterly Journal of Speech**, Vol. 90, No. 2, May, pp. 189–211.

Audier, Serge (2006), **Cumhuriyet Kuramları**, Trans. İsmail Yerguz, İletişim Yayınları, İstanbul.

Balibar, Etienne (2016), **Yurttaşlık**, Trans. Murat Erşen, Monokl Yayınevi, İstanbul.

Bauman, Zygmunt (1999), **Sosyolojik Düşünmek**, Trans. Abdullah Yılmaz, Ayrıntı Yayınları, İstanbul.

Baumann, Gerd (2016), "Çok-Kültürlülük (Multiculturalism)", Trans. Mehmet Karataş, **Sosyal Bilimler Ansiklopedisi 'İkinci Kitap/ A-K'**, Edit. Adam Kuper-Jessica Kuper, Adres Yayınları, Ankara, pp. 217–223).

Bauman, Zygmunt (2018), **Özgürlük**, Trans. Kübra Eren, Ayrıntı Yayınları, İstanbul.

Bauman, Zygmunt (2019), **Kimlik**, Trans. Mesut Hazır, Heretik Basın Yayın, Ankara.

Bellamy, Richard (1992), **Liberalism and Modern Society: An Historical Argument**, Polity Press, Cambridge & Oxford & Boston.

Bellamy, Richard (2015), "Citizenship: Historical Development of", Edited by James D. Wright, **International Encyclopedia of the Social & Behavioral Sciences, Volume: 3**, Elsevier Science & Technology, Oxford, pp. 1–18.

Benhabib, Seyla (2009), "Twilight of Sovereignty or the Emergence of Cosmopolitan Norms? Rethinking Citizenship in Volatile Times", Edited by Engin F. Isin, Peter Nyers, and Bryan S. Turner, **Citizenship Between Past and Future**, Routledge Taylor & Francis Group, London and New York, pp. 18–35.

Beriş, Hamit Emrah (2016), "Fransız Devrimi", Edit. Hamit Emrah Beriş-Fatih Duman, Siyasal Düşünceler Tarihi, Orion Kitabevi, Ankara, pp. 639–676.

Berting, Jan (2017), Avrupa 'Miras, Meydan Okuma, Vaat', Trans. Hüsamettin İnaç, Liberte Yayınları, Ankara.

Bourgeois, Bernard (2003), "George Wilhelm Friedrich Hegel", Trans. İsmail, Yerguz, Siyaset Felsefesi Sözlüğü, (Edit. Philippe Raynaud ve Stéphane Rials), İletişim Yayınları, İstanbul, pp. 59–68.

Braudel, Fernand (2017), Kapitalizmin Kısa Tarihi, Trans. İsmail Yerguz, Say Yayınları, İstanbul.

Brett, Annabel S. (2011), "Yurttaş Hakları Tasavvurunun Gelişimi", Trans. Gökhan Aksay, Devletler ve Yurttaşlar, Edit. Quentin Skinner & Bo Strath, Türkiye İş Bankası Kültür Yayınları, İstanbul, pp. 113–131.

Brubaker, W. Rogers (2008), "Fransa ve Almanya'da Göç, Vatandaşlık ve Ulus-Devlet: Karşılaştırmalı Bir Tarihsel Analiz", Trans. Can Cemgil, Vatandaşlığın Dönüşümü, (Edit. Ayşe Kadıoğlu), Metis Yayınları: İstanbul, pp. 55–92.

Buğra, Ayşe (2008), "Sosyal Haklar ve Eşit Vatandaşlık Kavramı", Edit. E. Fuat Keyman, Aydınlanma, Türkiye ve Vatandaşlık, Osmanlı Bankası Arşiv ve Araştırma Merkezi Yayınları, İstanbul, pp. 159–169.

Canfora, Luciano (2003), Demokratik Retoriğin Eleştirisi, Trans. Durdu Kundakçı, Dost Kitabevi Yayınları, Ankara.

Carnoy, Martin (2014), Devlet ve Siyaset Teorisi, Trans. Simten Coşar vd., Dipnot Yayınları, Ankara.

Caymaz, Birol (2007), Türkiye'de Vatandaşlık–Resmi İdeoloji ve Yansımaları-, İstanbul Bilgi Üniversitesi Yayınları, İstanbul.

Çelik, Fikret (2012), "Antik Çağ ve Rönesans'da Gelişen 'Evrensel Yurttaşlık' Anlayışının Modern Dönemdeki Yansıması: Fransız Yurttaşlığı", Düşünce Dünyasında Türkiz Siyaset ve Kültür Dergisi, Yıl: 3, Sayı: 13, pp. 88–104.

Dagger, Richard (1997), Civic Virtues, Rights, Citizenship and Republican Liberalism, Oxford University Press, Oxford.

Dahl, Robert A. (2018), Siyasi Eşitlik Üzerine, Trans. A. Emre Zeybekoğlu, Dost Kitabevi, Ankara.

Dahrendorf, Ralf (2015), **Demokrasinin Bunalımları**, Trans. A. Emre Zeybekoğlu, İthaki Yayınları, İstanbul.

Dauenhauer, Bernard P. (2001), **Kırılgan Bir Dünyada Yurttaşlık**, Trans. Ayşe Özdil-Filiz Kaynak, Çukurova Üniversitesi Basımevi, Adana.

de Lara, Philippe (2003), "Komünote ve Komünoteryanizm", Trans. İsmail, Yerguz, **Siyaset Felsefesi Sözlüğü**, (Edit. Philippe Raynaud ve Stéphane Rials), İletişim Yayınları, İstanbul, pp. 513–519.

Demir, Ömer ve Acar, Mustafa (2002), **Sosyal Bilimler Sözlüğü**, Vadi Yayınları, Ankara.

Dinan, Desmond (edit.-2005), **Avrupa Birliği Ansiklopedisi 'İkinci Cilt H-Z'**, (Trans. Hale Akay), Kitap Yayınevi, İstanbul.

Dobson, Andrew (2011), "Devletler, Yurttaşlar ve Çevre", Trans. Gökhan Aksay, **Devletler ve Yurttaşlar**, Edit. Quentin Skinner & Bo Strath, Türkiye İş Bankası Kültür Yayınları, İstanbul, pp. 251–274.

Donald, James (2008), "Vatandaş ve Kent Aylağı", (Edit. Ayşe Kadıoğlu), **Vatandaşlığın Dönüşümü**, Metis Yayınları, İstanbul, pp. 140–166.

Dreyfus, Françoise (2007), **Bürokrasinin İcadı**, Trans. Işık Ergüden, İletişim Yayınları, İstanbul.

Dworkin, Ronald (2006), "Liberal Topluluk", Trans. Elif Ergezene, **Liberaller ve Cemaatçiler**, Edit. André Berten vd., Dost Kitabevi, Ankara, pp. 274–291.

Gordon, Andrew & Stack, Trevor (2007), "Citizenship Beyond the State: Thinking with Early Modern Citizenship in the Contemporary World", **Citizenship Studies**, Vol. 11, No. 2, May, pp. 117–133.

Güçlü, Abdülbaki vd. (2008), **Felsefe Sözlüğü**, Bilim ve Sanat Yayınları, Ankara.

Gündüz, Mustafa ve Ferhan Gündüz (2007), **Yurttaşlık Bilinci**, Anı Yayıncılık, Ankara.

Harvey, David (2001), "Sınıf İlişkileri, Sosyal Adalet ve Farklılık Politikası", (Trans. Sinan Kadir Çelik ve Ayça Atikoğlu), **Praksis Sosyal Bilimler Dergisi**, "Kent ve Kapitalizm" Sayısı, pp. 173–203.

Hayek, Friedrich A. V. (2008), "Siyasî Bir İdeal Olarak Hukuk Devleti", Trans. Sevda Gültekin Göktolga-Ali Rıza Çoban, **Hukuk Devleti**

'Hukukî Bir İlke Siyasî Bir İdeal', Edit. Adnan Küçük vd., Adres Yayınları, Ankara, 2008, pp. 41–118.

Heater, Derek (2007), **Yurttaşlığın Kısa Tarihi**, Trans. Meral Delikara Üst, İmge Kitabevi, Ankara.

Heywood, Andrew (2012), **Siyasetin Temel Kavramları**, Trans. Hayrettin Özler, Adres Yayınları, Ankara.

Heywood, Andrew (2013), **Küresel Siyaset**, Trans. Nasuh Uslu & Haluk Özdemir, Adres Yayınları, Ankara.

Hindley, Geoffrey (edit.-1990), **The Book of Magna Carta**, Constable & Robinson Ltd., London.

Honderich, Ted (edit.-1995), **The Oxford Companion to Philosohy**, Oxford University Press, Oxford, London.

Honohan, Iseult (2017), "Liberal and Republican Conceptions of Citizenship", Edited by Ayelet Shachar vd., **Oxford Handbook of Citizenship**, Oxford University Press, Oxford, pp. 1–27.

Höfert, Almut (2011), "Geç Ortaçağda Devletler, Kentler ve Yurttaşlar", Trans. Gökhan Aksay, **Devletler ve Yurttaşlar**, Edit. Quentin Skinner & Bo Strath, Türkiye İş Bankası Kültür Yayınları, İstanbul, pp. 73–88.

Isin, Engin F. & Turner, Bryan S. (2009), "Investigating Citizenship: An Agenda for Citizenship Studies", Edited by Engin F. Isin, Peter Nyers, and Bryan S. Turner, **Citizenship Between Past and Future**, Routledge Taylor & Francis Group, London and New York, pp. 5–17.

Janoski, Thomas (1998), **Citizenship and Civil Society: A Framework of Rights and Obligations in Liberal, Traditional, and Social Democratic Regimes**, Cambridge University Press, Cambridge.

Jaume, Lucien (2003), "Yurttaşlık (Citizenship)", Trans. İsmail Yerguz, **Siyaset Felsefesi Sözlüğü**, Edit. Philippe Raynaud-Stéphane Rials, İletişim Yayınları, İstanbul, pp. 992–997.

Joppke, Christian (2009), "Transformation of Citizenship: Status, Rights, Identity", Edited by Engin F. Isin, Peter Nyers, and Bryan S. Turner, **Citizenship Between Past and Future**, Routledge Taylor & Francis Group, London and New York, pp. 36–47.

Joyce, Paul (1999), **Strategic Management for the Public Services**, Open University Press, Buckingham.

Kadıoğlu, Ayşe (2008a), "Vatandaşlığın Ulustan Arındırılması: Türkiye Örneği", (Edit. Ayşe Kadıoğlu), Vatandaşlığın Dönüşümü, Metis Yayınları, İstanbul, pp. 31–54.

Kadıoğlu, Ayşe (2008b), "Aydınlanma, Vatandaşlık ve Kadın: Türkiye Örneği", Edit. E. Fuat Keyman, Aydınlanma, Türkiye ve Vatandaşlık, Osmanlı Bankası Arşiv ve Araştırma Merkezi Yayınları, İstanbul, pp. 83–95.

Kadıoğlu, Ayşe (2008c), "Vatandaşlık: Kavramın Farklı Anlamları", (Edit. Ayşe Kadıoğlu), Vatandaşlığın Dönüşümü, Metis Yayınları, İstanbul, pp. 21–30.

Kadıoğlu, Ayşe (2009), "Political Participation from a Citizenship Perspective", Middle East Law and Interdisciplinary Governance Journal, Vol. 1, No. 1, pp. 90–116.

Kapani, Münci (1993), Kamu Hürriyetleri, Yetkin Yayınları, Ankara.

Keyman, E. Fuat (2008), "Önsöz: Kimlik, Vatandaşlık ve Demokratikleşme Türkiye Örneği", Edit. E. Fuat Keyman, Aydınlanma, Türkiye ve Vatandaşlık, Osmanlı Bankası Arşiv ve Araştırma Merkezi Yayınları, İstanbul, pp. 7–17.

Kymlicka, Will (1998), Çokkültürlü Yurttaşlık, Trans. Abdullah Yılmaz, Ayrıntı Yayınları: İstanbul.

Kymlicka, Will ve Wayne Norman (2008), "Vatandaşın Dönüşü: Vatandaşlık Kuramındaki Yeni Çalışmalar Üzerine Bir Değerlendirme", (Edit. Ayşe Kadıoğlu), Vatandaşlığın Dönüşümü, Metis Yayınları, İstanbul, pp. 185–217.

Labarriére, Jean-Louis (2003), "Erdem (Virtue)", Trans. İsmail Yerguz, Siyaset Felsefesi Sözlüğü, Edit. Philippe Raynaud-Stéphane Rials, İletişim Yayınları, İstanbul, pp. 305–312.

Lecoq, Jean-François (2003), "Roma Antikitesi (Roman Antiquity)", Trans. İsmail Yerguz, Siyaset Felsefesi Sözlüğü, Edit. Philippe Raynaud-Stéphane Rials, İletişim Yayınları, İstanbul, pp. 717–724.

Machiavelli, Niccolo (1998), Discourses on Livy, Translated by Harvey C. Mansfield and Nathan Tarcov, The University of Chicago Press, Chicago & London.

Margalit, Avishai & Raz, Joseph (1990), "National Self-Determination", The Journal of Philosophy, Vol. 87, No. 9, September, pp. 439–461.

Marshall, Gordon (1999), **Sosyoloji Sözlüğü** (Sociology Dictionary), Trans. Osman Akınhay-Derya Kömürcü, Bilim ve Sanat Yayınları, Ankara.

Marshall, Thomas Humprey ve T. Bottomore (2000), **Yurttaşlık ve Toplumsal Sınıflar**, Trans. Ayhan Kaya, Gündoğan Yayınları, Ankara.

Melnik, Stefan (2006), **Özgürlük, Refah ve Demokrasi Mücadelesi**, Trans. Atilla Yayla, Liberte Yayınları, Ankara.

Miller, David, vd. (1995), **Blackwell'in Siyasal Düşünce Ansiklopedisi II (K-Z)**, Trans. Bülent Paker-Nevzat Kıraç, Ümit Yayıncılık, Ankara.

Mindus, Patricia (2009), "The Contemporary Debate on Citizenship", **Journal for Constitutional Theory and Philosophy of Law**, Vol. 9, January, pp. 29–44.

Mooers, Colin (2000), **Burjuva Avrupa'nın Kuruluşu**, Trans. Bahadır Sina Şener, Dost Kitabevi, Ankara.

Moore, Barrington Jr. (2003), **Diktatörlüğün ve Demokrasinin Toplumsal Kökenleri**, Trans. Şirin Tekeli-Alaeddin Şenel, İmge Kitabevi, Ankara.

Müller, Jan-Werner (2012), **Anayasal Yurtseverlik**, Trans. A. Emre Zeybekoğlu, Dost Kitabevi, Ankara.

Oldfield, Adrian (2008), "Vatandaşlık: Doğal Olmayan Bir Pratik mi?", (Edit. Ayşe Kadıoğlu), **Vatandaşlığın Dönüşümü**, Metis Yayınları, İstanbul, pp. 93–106.

Özalp, Ahmet (2009), "Yoksulluk, Yoksunluk, Yurttaşlık: Sosyal Hak(sızlık)ları Politik Düşünmek", https://www.academia. edu/1352472/Yoksulluk_Yoksunluk_Yurtta%C5%9Fl%C4%B1k_ Sosyal_Hak_s%C4%B1zl%C4%B1k_lar%C4%B1_Politik_D%C3% BC%C5%9F%C3%BCnmek , pp. 276–284, 14.09.2020, 19:00.

Pasquino, Pasquale (2003), "Komünote ve Toplum (Communote and Society)", Trans. İsmail, Yerguz, **Siyaset Felsefesi Sözlüğü**, (Edit. Philippe Raynaud ve Stéphane Rials), İletişim Yayınları, İstanbul, pp. 519–522.

Pettit, Philip (1998), **Cumhuriyetçilik**, Trans. Abdullah Yılmaz, Ayrıntı Yayınları: İstanbul.

Philonenko, Alexis (2003), "Emmanuel Kant", Trans. İsmail, Yerguz, **Siyaset Felsefesi Sözlüğü**, (Edit. Philippe Raynaud ve Stéphane Rials), İletişim Yayınları, İstanbul, pp. 491–503.

Pocock, J. G. A. (1975), **The Machiavellian Momemt 'Florentine Political Thought and the Atlantic Republican Tradition'**, Princeton University Press, New Jersey.

Pocock, J. G. A. (1998), "The Ideal of Citizenship Since the Classical Times", Edited by Gershon Shafir, **The Citizenship Debates: A Reader**, University of Minnesota Press, Minneapolis & London, pp. 31–41.

Poggi, Gianfranco (1991), **Çağdaş Devletin Gelişimi 'Sosyolojik Bir Yaklaşım'**, Trans. Şule Kut-Binnaz Toprak, Hürriyet Vakfı Yayınları, İstanbul.

Poggi, Gianfranco (2011), "Yurttaşlar ve Devlet: Geçmişe Bakış ve Muhtemel Gelecek", Trans. Gökhan Aksay, **Devletler ve Yurttaşlar**, Edit. Quentin Skinner & Bo Strath, Türkiye İş Bankası Kültür Yayınları, İstanbul, pp. 39–52.

Polanyi, Karl (2006), **Büyük Dönüşüm 'Çağımızın Siyasal ve Ekonomik Kökenleri'**, Trans. Ayşe Buğra, İletişim Yayınları, İstanbul.

Rawls, John (2006), "Temel Özgürlükler ve Öncelikleri", Trans. Başak Demir, **Liberaller ve Cemaatçiler**, Edit.André Berten vd., Dost Kitabevi, Ankara, pp. 145–172.

Raz, Joseph (2008), "Hukuk Devleti ve Erdemi", Trans. Bilal Canatan, **Hukuk Devleti 'Hukukî Bir İlke Siyasî Bir İdeal'**, Edit. Adnan Küçük vd., Adres Yayınları, Ankara, pp. 149–166.

Roskin, Michael G. vd. (2013), **Siyaset Bilimi**, Trans. Atilla Yayla, Adres Yayınları, Ankara.

Ryan, Magnus (2011), "Özgürlük, Hukuk ve Ortaçağ Devleti", Trans. Gökhan Aksay, **Devletler ve Yurttaşlar**, Edit. Quentin Skinner & Bo Strath, Türkiye İş Bankası Kültür Yayınları, İstanbul, pp. 55–71.

Sabine, George H. (1965), **A History of Political Theory**, Holt, Rinehart and Winston INC., USA.

Sandel, Michael (2006), "Usuli Cumhuriyet ve Yükümsüz Ben", Trans. Eylem Özkaya, **Liberaller ve Cemaatçiler**, Edit. André Berten vd., Dost Kitabevi, Ankara, pp. 209–225.

Sartori, Giovanni (1996), **Demokrasi Teorisine Geri Dönüş**, Trans. Tunçer Karamustafaoğlu-Mehmet Turhan, Yetkin Basım Yayım ve Dağıtım, Ankara.

Schama, Simon (2015), **Yurttaşlar**, Trans. Ahmet Fethi, Alfa Basım Yayım, İstanbul.

Schnapper, Dominique (1995), **Yurttaşlar Cemaati 'Modern Ulus Fikrine Doğru'**, Trans. Özlem Okur, Kesit Yayıncılık, İstanbul.

Sennett, Richard (2017), **Otorite**, Trans. Kamil Duran, Ayrıntı Yayınları, İstanbul.

Skeat, Walter William (1985), **An Etymological Dictionary of the English Language**, Andesite Press, New York.

Skinner, Quentin (2004), **Machiavelli**, Trans. Cemal Atila, Altın Kitaplar Yayınevi, İstanbul.

Skinner, Quentin (2006), "Adalet, Kamu Yararı ve Özgürlüğün Önceliği Üzerine", Trans. Sedef Koç, **Liberaller ve Cemaatçiler**, Edit. André Berten vd., Dost Kitabevi, Ankara, pp. 173–187.

Skinner, Quentin (2014), **Modern Siyasal Düşüncenin Temelleri 'Birinci Cilt: Rönesans'**, Trans. Eren Buğralılar-Barış Yıldırım, Phoenix Yayınevi, Ankara.

Skinner, Quentin (2017), **Liberalizmden Önce Özgürlük**, Trans. Kemal Özdil, Islık Yayınları, İstanbul.

Skocpol, Theda (2004), **Devletler ve Toplumsal Devrimler**, Trans. S. Erdem Türközü, İmge Kitabevi, Ankara.

Spitz, Jean-Fabien (2003), "Yurttaşlık Hümanizması (Civic Humanism)", Trans. İsmail Yerguz, **Siyaset Felsefesi Sözlüğü**, Edit. Philippe Raynaud-Stéphane Rials, İletişim Yayınları, İstanbul, pp. 997–1004.

Strath, Bo (2011), "Devlet ve Devlete Yönelik Eleştiriler: Post-modern Bir Meydan Okumadan Söz Edilebilir Mi?", Trans. Gökhan Aksay, **Devletler ve Yurttaşlar**, Edit. Quentin Skinner & Bo Strath, Türkiye İş Bankası Kültür Yayınları, İstanbul, pp. 199–228.

Strauss, Leo (2011), **Doğal Hak ve Tarih**, Trans. Murat Erşen-Petek Onur, Say Yayınları, İstanbul.

Taylor, Charles (2006), **Modern Toplumsal Tahayyüller**, Trans. Hamide Koyukan, Metis yayınları, İstanbul.

Theodorakis, Katja (2014), "Refugees, Citizens and Nation-State: Unrecognised Anomalies and the need for New Political Imaginaries", The ANU Undergraduate Research Journal, Vol. 6, Canberra, pp. 37–48.

Tilly, Charles (2008), Toplumsal Hareketler, Trans. Orhan Düz, Babil Yayınları, İstanbul.

Touraine, Alain (2002), Eşitliklerimizle ve Farklılıklarımızla Birlikte Yaşayabilecek Miyiz?, Trans. Olcay Kunal, Yapı Kredi Yayınları, İstanbul.

Trigeaud, Jean-Marc (2003), "Hukuk (Law)", Trans. İsmail Yerguz, Siyaset Felsefesi Sözlüğü, (Edit. Philippe Raynaud ve Stéphane Rials), İletişim Yayınları, İstanbul, pp. 383–396.

Troper, Michel (2011), "Hukuki Devlet Kuramı Üstüne", Trans. Özlem Günyol, Devlet Kuramı, Edit. Cemal Bâli Akal, Dost Kitabevi Yayınları, Ankara, pp. 341–356.

Turner, Bryan S. (2008), "Bir Vatandaşlık Kuramının Anahtarı", (Edit. Ayşe Kadıoğlu), Vatandaşlığın Dönüşümü, Metis Yayınları, İstanbul, pp. 107–139.

Turner, Bryan S. & Hamilton, Peter (1994), "General Commentary", Citizenship 'Critical Concepts' Volume I, Edited by Bryan S. Turner & Peter Hamilton, Routledge Press, London, pp. I–X.

Uygun, Oktay (2017), Demokrasi 'Tarihsel, Siyasal ve Felsefi Boyutları', On İki Levha Yayıncılık, İstanbul.

Üstel, Füsun (2005), "Makbul Vatandaş"ın Peşinde –II. Meşrutiyet'ten Bugüne Vatandaşlık Eğitimi-, İletişim Yayınları, İstanbul.

Vega, Judith A. (2011), "Aydınlanmanın Farklılıkları, Bugünün Kimlikleri", Trans. Gökhan Aksay, Devletler ve Yurttaşlar, Edit. Quentin Skinner & Bo Strath, Türkiye İş Bankası Kültür Yayınları, İstanbul, pp. 135–156.

Weinberg, James & Flinders, Matthew (2018), "Learning for Democracy: The Politics and Practice of Citizenship Education", British Educational Research Journal, Vol. 44, No. 4, August, pp. 573–592.

Wellmer, Albrecht (2006), "Demokratik Bir Kültürün Koşulları: Liberallerle Cemaatçiler Arasındaki Tartışma Üzerine",

Trans. Mehmet Zafer Üskül, **Liberaller ve Cemaatçiler**, Edit. André Berten vd., Dost Kitabevi, Ankara, pp. 305–323.

White, Stephen K. (2009), **The Ethos of a Late-Modern Citizenship**, Harvard University Press, Cambridge, Massachusetts and London.

Williams, Fiona (2016), "Refah Devleti (Welfare State)", Trans. Ahmet Kemal Bayram, **Sosyal Bilimler Ansiklopedisi 'İkinci Kitap/L-Z'**, Edit. Adam Kuper-Jessica Kuper, Adres Yayınları, Ankara, pp. 1154–1157.

Yeatman, Anna (2009), "The Subject of Citizenship", **Citizenship Between Past and Future**, Edited by Engin F. Isin, Peter Nyers, and Bryan S. Turner, Routledge Taylor & Francis Group, London and New York, pp. 102–112.